Do You Make These Mistakes in English?

EDWIN L. BATTISTELLA

Do You Make These Mistakes in English?

The Story of Sherwin Cody's Famous Language School

OXFORD
UNIVERSITY PRESS
2009

OXFORD
UNIVERSITY PRESS

Oxford University Press, Inc., publishes works that further
Oxford University's objective of excellence
in research, scholarship, and education.

Oxford New York
Auckland Cape Town Dar es Salaam Hong Kong Karachi
Kuala Lumpur Madrid Melbourne Mexico City Nairobi
New Delhi Shanghai Taipei Toronto

With offices in
Argentina Austria Brazil Chile Czech Republic France Greece
Guatemala Hungary Italy Japan Poland Portugal Singapore
South Korea Switzerland Thailand Turkey Ukraine Vietnam

Published by Oxford University Press, Inc.
198 Madison Avenue, New York, New York 10016

www.oup.com

Oxford is a registered trademark of Oxford University Press

Library of Congress Cataloging-in-Publication Data
Battistella, Edwin L.
Do you make these mistakes in English? : the story of Sherwin Cody's
famous language school / Edwin L. Battistella.
p. cm.
ISBN 978-0-19-536712-6
1. Cody, Sherwin, 1868–1959. 2. English teachers—United States—Biography.
3. Entrepreneurs—United States—Biography. 4. Language and culture—United
States—History—20th century. 5. Correspondence schools and courses—History—
20th century. 6. English language—Rhetoric—Study and teaching. I. Title.
PE64.C64B38 2008
428.0071'50973—dc22 2007044652

9 8 7 6 5 4 3 2 1

Printed in the United States of America
on acid-free paper

Contents

Introduction

I FIRST BECAME AWARE OF SHERWIN CODY MANY YEARS ago from an advertisement in a comic book. The small ad was on the same page as the ones for X-ray specs, sea monkeys, joy buzzers, and ventriloquism pamphlets. The exact wording escapes me, but it promised mastery of the English language for just a couple of dollars. In the post-Sputnik meritocracy of the 1960s, that seemed like a good deal, and I ordered the set of pocket books through the mail. I even read them a bit at a time over a summer, along with more comic books.

Much later, and after much more schooling, I came across Sherwin Cody again. I was researching attitudes about grammar for a book called *Bad Language: Are Some Words Better Than Others?* I showed my wife a vintage ad I had found for the Cody books, titled "Good English and Good Fortune Go Hand in Hand." We began to wonder whether anyone had done work on Cody's course or life. I found other ads, bought a set of the correspondence course booklets, and began to track down some of Cody's hundred-plus publications and information about his many business ventures. Soon I was hooked.

Cody's trail was to be found in paper ephemera. At the center was his signature ad which reminded readers about their mistakes in English. Cody's ad offered success-oriented readers a scientifically tested method to improve their English in just a few minutes a day, and the success of the ads made Cody an often-cited figure in the history of advertising. But he was largely unmentioned elsewhere—in linguistics, English studies, rhetoric, or the history of the book. Cody was not a member of the American literary elite and he was not a professional linguist. He was an entrepreneur—a businessman and business teacher whose success was in mass-marketing good English and in building a correspondence school that helped over 150,000 men and women improve their speech and writing. Cody saw himself as an independent scholar and applied scientist as well, and his goal was to blend the practical and the intellectual, a goal we sometimes seem to give up on today. Cody addressed many concerns in his writings, and his work as a whole should be considered part of American success and self-help rhetoric. And the central practical issue that Cody grappled with was one that has always been at the heart of language study: how we are judged by our speech and writing.

Acknowledgments

THIS RESEARCH BENEFITED FROM THE GENEROUS HELP OF many institutions and individuals. The National Endowment for the Humanities provided a valuable summer research stipend (FT-5327405), which was followed by a sabbatical leave from Southern Oregon University during which the manuscript was completed.

I received research help from many people, near and far. Members of the Cody family were generous with their time and recollections: Peter Malcolm Cody of Maryland, Professor Gabrielle Hamilton Cody of New York, and Aldus M. Cody of Florida. Rutgers University business professor Carter A. Daniel shared recollections of his interviews with Morrill Cody and provided valuable advice and comments along the way.

History researcher Ben Truwe of Medford, Oregon, Sara Rogers of the Dobbs Ferry Public Library, Robert Scheffel of the local history division of the Central Library of Rochester and Monroe County, Molly O'Hagen Hardy of the Harry Ransom Humanities Research Center, Barbara Simmons of the Amherst College Library, Georgette Hedberg of the Dobbs Ferry Historical Society, Cynthia Soroka of Charles Atlas Ltd., and Paul Collins of Gracion Software also provided helpful information along the way, and librarian Jim Rible assisted in the preparation of some of the images reproduced here. Anna Beauchamp, interlibrary loan librarian at the Lenn and Dixie Hannon Library, went above and beyond the call of duty helping me to track down old, odd, and unusual references and Cody's publications and advertisements.

The images from Cody's ads, prospectus, and course are reproduced with the permission of Peter M. Cody and Gabrielle Hamilton Cody. The "Creative Man's Corner" in Chapter 15 is reproduced with the permission of Crain Communications, Inc.

I am also indebted to the fine referees for Oxford University Press for their comments and to Maureen Flanagan for her reality check on the final version and for her help in pixel editing. Special thanks to Executive Editor Peter Ohlin of Oxford University Press for his work in bringing this project to fruition.

A note on the citations to *The 100% Self-correcting Course in English Language*: the booklets are unpaginated and contain both regular two-sided pages and tri-fold pages with two regular sides and material repeated for a second trial of a lesson. I have adopted the convention of citing pages without counting the extra folds. So a citation of *Lesson 1, 3* refers to the first booklet and the third regular page.

Do You Make These Mistakes in English?

ONE

An Advertisement That Never Changed

In the early 1900s the average life expectancy in the United States was under 50 years. Catastrophic fires and mine explosions were common, and there were still outbreaks of typhoid and the bubonic plague. Few Americans graduated from high school, two out of every ten adults couldn't read or write, and unskilled workers made between $200 and $400 a year. The Ford Motor Company and the World Series were just getting started. Andrew Carnegie, the Bill Gates of his day, was building the Carnegie Institute in Pittsburgh and funding about 2,000 Carnegie libraries across the nation. And a balding, middle-aged writer named Sherwin Cody was marketing a home-study course on *The Art of Writing and Speaking the English Language.*

Cody would eventually develop a correspondence version of his course that would last for over 40 years. Together with the Harvard Classics, *The Book of Etiquette,* the Book-of-the-Month Club, and other mail-order products, Sherwin Cody's *100% Self-correcting Course in English Language* introduced working-class and middle-class consumers to the skills, manners, and mental habits of the successful. Cody's course had a signature advertisement that was just as durable, and even gained cult status over the years—he asked "Do You Make These Mistakes in English?"[1]

The headline offered free information about English, promising to reveal *mistakes* that *you* may be making and appealing to readers' insecurities about language. The typical ad copy led off with several examples of mistakes in English. Some were simple spelling and grammatical errors (*calander, you was*) while others were less obvious, such as Cody's preference for *Have you heard from him today?* over *Did you hear from him today?*[2] The ads offered a patented self-correcting device to provide improvement in just 15 minutes a day and promised more astonishing facts about English in a free prospectus.

Longer ads also explained why so many people were deficient in English, citing the "crying disgrace" of the nation's schools, and detailed Cody's credentials. They explained that the scientifically tested device to correct one's bad habits was "Mr. Cody's voice behind you, ready to speak out whenever you commit an error" and assured the reader that Cody would be a patient "everlasting mentor beside you, a mentor who would not laugh at you, but who would, on the contrary, support and help you."[3] The ads also explained how the system was efficient. Cody's system identified personal mistakes and concentrated on those so "You do not need to study anything you already know." Ads also emphasized Cody's research in simplifying grammar to essentials, letting readers know that "statistics show that a list of sixty words . . . make up more than half our speech and letter writing" and that only 25 errors in grammar make up 90 percent of mistakes. This was not the old grammar of obscure rules and technical terms. It was a modern, personalized, scientific system. The longer ads were also direct about the social and financial value of good English. Cody's students would gain "a facility in speech that marks them as educated people in whatever society they find themselves." And there was the offer of a free lesson. Readers could clip a coupon to receive a free book telling "one of the most interesting stories about English that ever has been written."

Do You Make These Mistakes in English?

Sherwin Cody's remarkable invention has enabled more than 115,000 people to correct their mistakes in English. Only 15 minutes a day required to improve your speech and writing.

MANY persons say, "Did you hear from him today?" They should say, "Have you heard from him today?" Some spell "calendar" "calender" or "calander." Still others say "between you and I" instead of "between you and me." It is astonishing how often "who" is used for "whom," and how frequently the simplest words are mispronounced. Few know whether to spell certain words with one or two "c's," or "m's," or "r's," or with "ie" or "ei." Most persons use only common words—colorless, flat, ordinary. Their speech and their letters are lifeless, monotonous, humdrum.

Every time they talk or write they show themselves lacking in the essential points of English.

Wonderful New Invention

For many years Mr. Cody studied the problem of creating instinctive habits of using good English. After countless experiments he finally invented a simple method by which you can acquire a better command of the English language in only 15 minutes a day. Now you can stop making the mistakes which have been hurting you. Mr. Cody's students have secured more improvement in five weeks than previously had been obtained by other pupils in two years!

Learn by Habit—Not by Rules

Under old methods rules are memorized, but correct habits are not formed. Finally the rules themselves are forgotten. The new Sherwin Cody method provides for the formation of correct habits by calling to your attention constantly only the *mistakes you yourself make*.

One of the wonderful things about Mr. Cody's course is the speed with which these habit-forming practice drills can be carried out. You can write the answers to fifty questions in 15 minutes and correct your work in 5 minutes more. The drudgery and work of copying have been ended by Mr. Cody! You concentrate always on your own mistakes until it becomes "second nature" to speak and write correctly.

SHERWIN CODY

FREE—Book On English

A new book explaining Mr. Cody's remarkable method is ready. If you are ever embarrassed by mistakes in grammar, spelling, punctuation, pronunciation, or if you cannot instantly command the exact words with which to express your ideas, this new free book, "How You Can Master Good English—in 15 Minutes a Day," will prove a revelation to you. Send the coupon or a letter or postal card for it now. No agent will call. SHERWIN CODY SCHOOL OF ENGLISH, 60 Searle Building, Rochester, N. Y.

SHERWIN CODY SCHOOL OF ENGLISH,
60 Searle Building, Rochester, N. Y.

Please send me, without any obligation on my part, your new free book, "How You Can Master Good English—in 15 Minutes a Day."

Name..

Address..

....

☐ *If 18 years or under check here for Booklet A.*

FIGURE 1.1. An advertisement that never changed.

The Cody ad ran widely, appearing in magazines like *The American Magazine, The Ladies' Home Journal,* and *The World's Work,* in pulps like *Amazing Stories* and *Black Mask,* in annuals like *The World Almanac and Book of Facts,* in comic books, and in the Sunday newspaper book reviews and magazine supplements. Cody's ads began appearing in *The New York Times* in 1919 and ran two or three times a year until 1959, usually as a full page on the back of the book review or magazine. Over the years, however, Cody and the copywriters working on his account experimented with a number of headlines, including some that invited the reader to construct a narrative from a drawing or photo. For example, in "He thinks he is speaking correct English!" the drawing of the women looking at the speaker tells everything we need to know—that despite the suit and hat, the man on the telephone lacks refinement. Other headlines were accusatory imperatives to "Stop Making Mistakes in Speaking and Writing!" and "Stop Abusing the English Language!"

Cody and adman Victor Schwab experimented with variations on the "mistakes" theme, and they kept track of the return rate of various ads and placements as they adjusted their marketing buys. The "Do You Make These Mistakes in English?" version of the ad was the most often used and the most successful. Over the years, the number of students served was updated, going from "thousands" in the mid-1920s to 150,000 in the 1950s. Pictures, drawings, sidebar, and new testimonials were inserted on occasion, but most often the ad had a single image of Cody, bearded and balding, looking from the middle of the page toward its left column of text.

As we shall see, there was more to the course than the brief pitch provided in the advertisements, and more to Sherwin Cody as well. This book aims to place Cody's work—his advertising campaign, his course, his "scientific" approach, and his philosophy of life—in the cultural context of the first half of the twentieth century. Why is this important? Or to frame the question as Cody

He *thinks* he is speaking Correct English!

Can you find his FIVE mistakes?

IF you were introduced to an attractive, prosperous-looking man or woman who constantly made crude mistakes in grammar and pronunciation, what would you think? You could not *help* thinking that this person was sadly lacking in education; you would feel that he or she belonged on a lower social level.

And yet, unless you have made the correctness of your own speech a *habit,* you never can be sure that you are not unconsciously making errors which may cause others to lower their estimates of your education and refinement.

You may not make such glaring errors as *I ain't, you was,* and *between you and I,* but perhaps you commit other mistakes which offend the ears of those who know, and cause them to judge you unfairly.

If you *are* making slips in speech or writing, you will never learn about them from those who notice them, for your friends are too polite to criticize your English to your face.

Perhaps you sometimes use *who* for *whom,* or *would* for *should.* Are you always sure whether to spell words with one or two "c's" or "m's" or "r's" or with "ei" or "ie"? Are you sure that you never say, "I did it already"—or "He don't mean what he says"?

What Can You Do?

For many years Sherwin Cody studied the problem of creating the habit of using good English. He found that under old methods, rules are memorized, but correct habits are not formed. Soon the rules themselves are forgotten. The new Sherwin Cody method provides, on the contrary, for the formation of correct habits by constantly calling attention only to the mistakes you make—and then showing you the right way, so that correct English soon becomes "second nature." Already over 70,000 people have used this method with the most marked results.

Free Booklet on English

A new booklet explaining Mr. Cody's invention is ready. If you are ever embarrassed by mistakes in grammar, spelling, punctuation, pronunciation, or if your vocabulary is limited, this new free booklet, "How You Can Master Good English in 15 Minutes a Day," will prove a revelation to you. Send the coupon or a letter or postal card for it now. SHERWIN CODY SCHOOL OF ENGLISH, 63 Searle Building, Rochester, N. Y.

SHERWIN CODY SCHOOL OF ENGLISH
63 Searle Building, Rochester, N. Y.

Please send me your free booklet "How You Can Master Good English in 15 Minutes a Day."

Name ....

Address ....

....

This valuable booklet can not be sent to children.

FIGURE 1.2. A Cody ad from the 1930s.

might have: Why should you be interested in the Sherwin Cody School of English?

If you have studied marketing, Cody's name may be familiar to you as an advertising pioneer and a client-collaborator of the legendary admen Maxwell Sackheim and Victor Schwab. And if you have studied professional writing, Cody may be a footnote figure in discussions of the cardinal C's of business communication (correctness, clarity, conciseness, courtesy, coherence, and character). We look at these roles of Cody's and also at the advertising of correctness in English. Sherwin Cody's course provides a long-running case study of the way in which the early twentieth-century mass media and advertising marketed self-improvement and sold correct behavior, and we will place Cody's course within the larger genre that included the Harvard Classics and the Book-of-the-Month Club, Dale Carnegie's advice on winning friends and influencing people, and even the body-building prescriptions of Charles Atlas. Taken together, this self-improvement advertising reflects techniques, narratives, and themes—anxiety about social judgment and desire for success—that were successful during a much earlier information and media revolution. By understanding Sherwin Cody's marketing of English in the context of the marketing of self-improvement, we gain perspective not just on the history of marketing but on some of the advertising that we encounter today.

Cody's story is also one for grammarians, linguists, and English educators. Language scholars may have a passing recognition of Sherwin Cody from his ads. But if you judge Cody merely by his ads, you are likely to dismiss him as scoldingly traditional, or worse. A fuller look at his work reveals that Cody was a modern grammarian who generally advocated colloquial over bookish usage. He was also a practical grammarian who aimed at simplifying grammar instruction so it could be taught efficiently and in relation to individual weaknesses. For linguists and English teachers, Cody's story reveals to us the ways that modern ideas about grammar and teaching emerge in unexpected places and the way that traditional grammar evolved to practical rules for correcting the most common errors.

Cody's course and his ad campaign also speak to language scholars in another way. They highlight grammar as a symbol of the social dynamics of correctness. We are anxious to appear educated, but also anxious not to be so educated as to be pedantic or stuffy. Cody claimed this colloquial middle ground for language, literature, and culture, and his orientation fit new working-class and middle-class attitudes. The classic liberal arts education that Cody himself had received was being challenged by newer forms of study, and Cody himself had mixed feelings about the value of that education. He saw the literary style in speech as outmoded and crafted a practical twentieth-century message. Good speaking, good writing, and good reading were a passport to success and fulfillment, but grammar rules and reading lists needed to be modern and pruned of deadwood.

Today's educators will also find Cody's role as an educational critic of interest. As Cody built a business career as a teacher and textbook publisher, he became an advocate of educational testing, founding a national organization of schools of business and proposing an efficient employment registry. He was part of an idealistic group of civic leaders and school efficiency consultants who sought to make schools more businesslike and accountable and who saw a new partnership between schools and employers based on the science of testing. Cody's work thus provides historical context for those of us who grapple with present-day assessment and standards models.

Cody's story is also about the education of workers and place-bound students. If we think of the early twentieth-century postal service as the internet of its day, Cody's course involved distance education for nontraditional students. As an educational critic and entrepreneur, Cody was naturally drawn to the emerging business model of correspondence education, which was becoming popular in universities and as private business. His experiences in this new field tell us something about the potential for online education today, which faces similar challenges and reactions.

Sherwin Cody's interests were broader than just one field. Like many successful entrepreneurs, he worked across boundaries, carrying ideas from one area to another. We often hear today that the average person changes careers several times and that those entering college will end up in types of work that don't yet quite exist. Cody's story illustrates someone making such transitions a century ago. His entrepreneurship was set in the context of the social, cultural, and economic forces of his time, but many of these forces remain today—advertising, mass culture, self-improvement, educational efficiency—and so Sherwin Cody's experience has relevance in our twenty-first-century world. Because he lived nearly a century, Cody's story is also part of America's story. He was born at the passing of the Fourteenth Amendment and the impeachment of Andrew Johnson and he lived until the statehood of Alaska and Hawaii and the beginnings of the U.S. space program. In looking closely at a life spanning such great changes in American society, business, and culture, we can learn more than the fine points of speaking and writing the English language.

This book is organized into 16 chapters. Chapters Two and Three recount Cody's early years, his attempt at a literary career, his entry into the publishing business, and his emergence as a critic of traditional education. Here we see the trajectory that led him to work in testing and eventually to the creation of his correspondence course. Chapter Four describes the emergence of the modern advertising industry and Cody's connection with Sackheim and Schwab as he developed a commercially viable correspondence course, an advertising campaign, and a marketing strategy for the *100% Self-correcting Course in English Language*. Chapters Five through Seven look at the course itself and its major themes—practical speaking, spelling and pronunciation, punctuation, grammar, vocabulary, and reading—and in Chapters

Five and Six you have an opportunity to test your knowledge of the English language with some of Cody's lessons. In Chapter Seven, Cody's advice on literature is discussed as an example of the role of book culture in self-improvement ideology.

Chapters Eight through Eleven look at some other, related self-improvement products popular in the first half of the twentieth century. Beginning with the narrative themes of print advertising, these chapters introduce the ad campaigns for the International Correspondence Schools, the Harvard Classics, the Book-of-the Month Club, *The Book of Etiquette,* the U.S. School of Music, the body-building course of Charles Atlas, and the self-confidence course of Dale Carnegie. Understanding these helps us to situate Cody's correspondence course in the rhetoric of conduct, success, and self-improvement and helps us to situate grammar as well.

Chapters Twelve through Fourteen analyze the market conditions that enabled Cody's course to grow and thrive. Here we take up American attitudes toward language and culture and look at the ways in which linguistic and rhetorical thought were evolving during Cody's time. We also look at the emergence of correspondence education as a means of serving workers, rural dwellers, and others to whom traditional university education was unavailable. Chapters Fifteen and Sixteen describe the last years of the *100% Self-correcting Course* in the 1950s and the combination of factors—personal, cultural, business, and demographic—that brought about its decline.

While the Sherwin Cody School of English has come and gone, its history is a window on language and culture. In this book we dust off that window.

TWO

From Literature to Business

To understand how Sherwin Cody came to develop his "remarkable new invention," we need to begin with a different question: who was Sherwin Cody? Alpheus Sherwin Cody was born in 1868, just a dozen miles from Grand Rapids, Michigan, where his parents, Aldus and Eliza, had moved from Ohio. Aldus Cody owned a sawmill and gristmill, and the family lived in a two-room, bark-covered cabin. There were a post office and grocery store nearby, and the area was known for a time as Cody's Mills. Sherwin Cody reports being born on a snowy Thanksgiving, November 30, and says he was glad he was "born like a real American pioneer."[1] According to Cody, both of his parents' families had New England roots, and his father left Oberlin College to join the Ohio volunteers fighting against slavery in the Civil War. Aldus had contracted tuberculosis while fighting in the war, and he and Eliza both found the Michigan winters hard. Soon after Sherwin was born, the family moved to Lincoln, Nebraska, where Aldus ran a hardware store and later bought a 40-acre fruit farm. He died when Sherwin was about ten, apparently from the recurring tuberculosis.

Eliza Cody was also educated, having studied first at Oberlin and during the Civil War at the Painesville Seminary. Though she never completed her studies, Cody described her as being strong in mathematics and as having an interest in languages. Sherwin was the oldest of four sons, and with four boys to educate, Eliza home-schooled at first. She also had plans for young Sherwin, intending for him to go two years to Oberlin and then to "some Eastern college [because] she wanted me to be better educated than my parents."[2] But Eliza too had been prone to illness, and she died about a year and a half after her husband, leaving Sherwin Cody and his younger brothers orphaned. Cody's maternal grandmother had lived with them and managed the household until the family could move to New Hampshire to be near other relatives.

The death of his parents, and especially of his mother, deeply affected Cody, so much so that in his running autobiography, he referred to her as his "guardian angel" and emphasized his promise to get a good education. Cody drove himself toward this goal of building a better life than his parents had. In New Hampshire, he attended the Canterbury district school and studied Latin privately with a Dartmouth-educated farmer. But Cody also needed to contribute to the household and could find little work in Canterbury. He located a boarding house in Waltham, Massachusetts, and with his grandmother's blessing moved there to finish high school. At Waltham High School, Cody distinguished himself in mathematics, founded a debate society, and was finally able to study Greek in his junior year. His next stop would be Amherst College.

WORKING HIS WAY THROUGH COLLEGE

Founded in 1821 by a committee that included lexicographer Noah Webster, Amherst College had a special mission to educate indigent young men, and 17-year-old Sherwin Cody certainly qualified when he arrived there in 1885. Cody chose Amherst "because of all the colleges in the country I decided I was likely to get the best education there."[3] Money was a constant worry, and Cody devoted two chapters of his autobiography to his college finances. He had received a small pension from the death of his father and some back pension money as well, and he managed to save about $115. But after paying his first year's tuition of $50 and renting a room for $10 for the year, Cody had little left to live on. He described how close he came to starvation in his first term in college, living on "potatoes and corn mush" with "a pint of milk a day, some bread, and an occasional egg."[4] His first year's expenses (including tuition) were $319, and he earned the difference by a variety of jobs.

Cody also received help from Julius Hawley Seelye, Amherst's president. Seelye was an Amherst graduate himself, who had worked as a missionary and as the pastor of the First Dutch Reformed Church in Schenectady, New York. In 1858 he returned to his alma mater as Professor of Philosophy, served as a member of Congress from 1875 to 1877, and assumed the presidency of Amherst in 1877. With Seelye's intervention, Cody received some financial support from an aunt who sent him ten dollars a month. Seelye also eventually hired Cody as his personal secretary, a job that helped Cody begin his career as an entrepreneur. The typewriter was just coming into mass production while Cody was in college, and he persuaded an uncle to advance him money to buy one for his job. Cody ended up acquiring a new Remington, which he also put to use in a class he was taking with rhetoric professor John Franklin Genung. Genung was lecturing from the notes to his soon-to-be-famous rhetoric text, and Cody offered to type and reproduce Genung's notes in advance for the class. To do this, Cody constructed a hectograph, an early form of duplicating machine that used a glycerin-coated plate of gelatin to make copies. He collected 75 cents each from a hundred students and reproduced Genung's notes as four-page leaflets. He reported that he "cleared twenty-five dollars on this first publishing operation," and he went on to make another eleven dollars copying a play for a nearby girls' school. By his sophomore year, Cody had received a scholarship, and he and another student even borrowed money to buy a boarding house. Becoming a property owner and landlord in his sophomore year provided sufficient financial security that Cody was able to devote his junior and senior years mostly to study.

His financial circumstances taught Cody entrepreneurship, but he was learning other things at Amherst as well. Cody's education was grounded in the traditional liberal arts and classics. He took a total of eleven courses in Latin and Greek, reading Catullus in Latin and Aeschylus, Euripides, and the New Testament in Greek. In philosophy, Cody read Huxley, Tyndall, Spencer, Berkeley, Kant, Conte, Hegel, and Swedenborg. He studied mathematics, philosophy, chemistry, and history, which included art history and which got him interested in "the great artists of the Renascence."[5] Reflecting on his education, however, Cody was ambivalent. In an essay called "What is the Value of a College Course?" he wrote that the classical aspects of college were valuable in acquainting students with the "great minds of all time" and helping to develop "some underlying principles that afterward [are] eternal." At the same time, Cody felt that college was oriented too much toward the past. "A college man," he wrote, "needs to take at once a course of applied science and philosophy and literature in the actual work of today. It is a pity he is not better prepared to do this, but stumbles on it blindly, in pained distress. Perhaps they do it better now than in my day."[6]

Cody was graduated from Amherst in 1889, at the age of 21. He had begun college seeing himself as an engineer but, in his first year, found himself increasingly drawn to literature. At Amherst he kept journals, begun partly in an attempt to learn to write with his left hand after he was confined to his room with an infection in his right hand. Journaling became a habit, and Cody wrote "confessions, philosophic discussions, love stories, prose poems, anything and everything." He reported writing for two to four hours a day and producing a total of about 2,400 pages during his college years—a dozen 200-page volumes stapled with loose-leaf covers. (Today he would doubtless be a blogger.) In his journals, Cody often imitated writers like De Quincey, Thackeray, Macaulay, and Shelley and even published student essays on Macaulay and De Quincey. But while he appreciated literary history, he later came to see the literary style as an impediment, claiming that the formal style "killed the sale of my writing for many years, till I wished I had never heard of college."[7]

LITERARY VAGABOND

On graduation from college, Cody worked as a teacher for a short while in Kingsport, Rhode Island, to pay off some college debts, but his real passion was to write. After his teaching stint, he found work as a reporter at the *Boston Herald* from 1889 to 1890, during which he interviewed Oliver Wendell Holmes, Sr. For a short time Cody was the private secretary to John Bigelow, one of the founders of the New York Public Library. From 1890 to 1892, he worked as a proofreader in a publishing house owned by William Eaton Chandler, who was a senator from New Hampshire, and in 1892 Cody also worked as Chandler's private secretary.[8] By 1893, when he was 25, Cody was in New York, conducting what he calls a literary apprenticeship. He wrote that "All this time I was carrying on my 'education in the world,' almost ready to forget I was ever a college man, and at the same time writing and rewriting a dozen volumes. . . ."[9] Cody described himself at this time as a "hack writer," and in one version of his *Story Writing and Journalism* volume, he recounted how he supported himself by preparing a history of the Chinese Empire in the wake of the Boxer Rebellion and by writing advertising booklets such as "How to Build a Cheap House."[10] Cody also wrote book reviews, earning money by reselling review copies to used bookstores, and he remarked that most books could be reviewed after reading just ten pages, and some after reading just ten lines or glancing at the contents page.[11]

In 1893 Cody privately published a series of love poems called *Life's Philosophy,* and in 1894 he published some lessons he had been using to teach story writing as a five-dollar book called *How to Write Fiction, Especially the Art of Short Story Writing*. It included discussion of different kinds of stories; methods for writing; advice on setting, character, theme, dialogue, plot, and style; and even suggestions on how to observe people. While the book was largely ignored, the Chicago *Dial* gave it such a laudatory review that Cody thought his reputation was made.[12]

From 1894 to 1896, Cody lived in London, where he sought to establish a literary career. He became a member of the New Vagabonds Club, and he republished *How to Write Fiction*. Cody also realized his ambition to publish a novel when J. M. Dent accepted *In the Heart of the Hills*. The novel tells the story of Alec Howe, the son of a prosperous New York merchant. After a dispute with his father and stepmother, Alec sets off to find his fortune in rural New Hampshire. He is befriended by a shopkeeper and his family, and Alec eventually comes to manage the store after the shopkeeper dies. Through hard work and business acumen, Alec becomes successful and marries. The novel ends, Horatio Alger–like, with financial success and local philanthropy:

> Alexander Howe is now the rich man of the town in Ashton. He made a considerable fortune in his business, and owns a large farm, which he intends turning into a private park,—private, but open to all his town's people.[13]

In the Heart of the Hills was a failure, however, and Cody's literary career stalled, causing him to reflect that "As an optimistic American I couldn't write for the old world British."[14] Cody did succeed in another way, however, marrying an English woman named Marian Teresa Hurley. Together they moved in 1896 to

Chicago, a city that Cody described as the frontier of literary civilization and that he perhaps saw as more promising for his future than New York or London. Chicago was where he would remain for the next 20 years as he completed his transition from literature to business.

HOW TO WRITE LETTERS THAT PULL

In Chicago, Cody returned to the newspaper business, working first at the *Chicago Record* and then at the *Chicago Tribune*. Correspondence education was coming into vogue at the recently founded University of Chicago, and the *Tribune* was offering home-study courses as well. Cody was put to work on the *Tribune*'s course on the English language. Of about a hundred courses offered, only two had any success, Cody's course on English and another course on bookkeeping. While at the *Tribune,* Cody also continued his literary work, publishing a book on *Story Composition* in 1897 and developing a relationship with the Werner School Book Company. In 1899 Cody produced biographical booklets on William Cullen Bryant, Washington Irving, Edgar Allan Poe, and John Greenleaf Whittier, as well as school books on *Four American Poets* (Bryant, Longfellow, Whittier, and Holmes) and *Four Famous American Writers* (Irving, Poe, James Russell Lowell, and Bayard Taylor).

As he became more involved in publishing, Cody had the idea of reissuing his *Tribune* home-study course in pocket-sized book form, and he solicited some advance orders from Sears, Roebuck and Company and from a Chicago correspondence school. By May of 1903, Cody had enough credit established to publish the books, and he set about marketing them in a Chicago-based business magazine called *The System* (which would much later become *Business Week*). Edward Thurnau, the advertising manager, offered Cody full-page ads on a profit-sharing basis, and in the period from 1903 to 1906 Cody sold about 25,000 sets of

The Art of Writing and Speaking the English Language this way.[15] By 1903, when Cody was 35, he had made the shift from literature to business.

Marketing his own books taught Cody about advertising. Early ads showed the books with their mundane individual titles: *Word Study, Grammar, Composition, Constructive Rhetoric.* Later ads depicted the books with descriptive titles like *Can you Spell? Grammar Simplified, Knack of Using Words,* and *Letter Writing/Story Writing.* Cody realized a good profit on *The Art of Writing and Speaking the English Language,* but more important was the knowledge he was gaining about business and marketing. He was also networking with businessmen and thinking ahead to new opportunities. *The Art of Writing and Speaking* had contained a chapter on writing a business letter, and Cody came to realize that

> the business men who bought my books on word study, grammar, and composition really wanted or needed to know the psychology of human appeal rather than the technicality of language. There was obviously a chance to sell these interested customers a correspondence course. I had been studying the common man as a reader of novels, and I found he was exactly the same person as the reader of business letters. I was therefore able to transfer my hard-earned knowledge of the psychology of literary appeal to business appeal, simply by a little practical adaptation.[16]

What he came up with was something called the Cody System. This was a set of 50 instruction cards for business writing, each mailed out weekly and sold as a course for $10. For a dollar down, a businessman could get the first several lessons and then decide whether to continue to pay for more lessons. Cody used an approach that would come to be known as "the negative option," telling readers that if the first lessons were not returned to Cody within a week, the course would be cancelled. (The negative option would later be adapted and made famous by the Book-of-the-Month Club.) Cody reported making about

FIGURE 2.1. An ad for the Cody letter-writing system.

$25,000 in the next three years, which he described as "the first easy money I ever made."[17]

Cody was also learning about correspondence education. He had begun to give personalized correspondence courses for $90, but he soon found that the work involved in individual instruction by mail far outweighed the pay. Nevertheless, the experience of working with 60 or so different businesses allowed him to test ideas in actual sales letters for businesses. He was able to find out which approaches sold and which didn't, noting that "Sales letters gave me an opportunity to measure results which few literary writers ever have."[18]

Business leaders were also becoming increasingly interested in school reform, and some of Cody's business clients suggested that he teach his system in the schools. Sensing a new opportunity and recognizing that magazine advertising to businessmen would be a finite market, Cody turned again to schoolbook publishing. He had established his own publishing imprint called The Old Greek Press in 1903, and he used it to publish a series of practical business guides. His textbook *Good English Form Book in Business Letter Writing* came out in 1904 and sold about 10,000 copies. A revision, tested in a YMCA adult-education class for secretaries, sold about 25,000 copies through the *System* magazine and another 125,000 to schools by mail order. In 1905 he published *Exercises in Word-Study,* and in 1906 he produced *Success in Letter Writing.* In 1908, he followed these with *How to Do Business by Letter.*

Cody did not give up the literary life entirely. In 1903 he published a short essay on Poe in the *Dial,* and he continued to publish literary anthologies such as *A Selection from the Best English Essays* and *The Best Tales of Edgar Allan Poe* (both in 1903). He followed these with two more anthologies in 1904 (*A Selection from the World's Great Orations* and *A Selection from the Great English Poets*) and a reading guide titled *How to Read and What to Read*. In 1907, Cody came out with a book series called the Nutshell Library, which was made up of separate volumes of excerpts from Longfellow, Poe, Dickens, and others, together with some biographical material. The books were marketed as an evening's reading; they would become an important auxiliary to his later correspondence course. As a publisher, Cody was learning about the schoolbook market, and he found that rural schools were a good market for his books, since urban areas tended to have more booksellers competing for orders. He was also learning his limitations. In 1906 he launched a humor magazine called *The Touchstone*. According to the announcement in *The New York Times, The Touchstone* described itself as "a human, sensible, amusing, critical review of the great world of women, literature, and the arts."[19] It lasted just five issues.

In the early 1900s, Sherwin Cody was finding his way in the world. He was blending his classical education with growing experience in the world of business—as a private secretary and a writer, as an advertiser and publisher, and as an entrepreneur. And he was applying the habits developed on his roundabout journey from Nebraska to Chicago—industriousness, resilience, drive, an eye for innovation, and an understanding of the business world. Despite his failure as a novelist, his self-image was strong, and he saw himself as ready to build a bridge between the literary world and the commercial world.

Cody on Business Letter Writing

What should a business letter do? Here is some advice from Cody's 1903 *Constructive Rhetoric* (pages 13–15 and 29–32):

- A business letter should be strictly grammatical
- The character of the person to whom the letter is to be sent wholly determines the form of the letter and even what is to be said
- Never write a longer letter than will be read
- The most important principle of composition for letter writers to master is condensation
- [Omit] all details that the recipient of the letter may reasonably be supposed to know already
- [Suggest and imply] in the choice of words and forms of sentences as much as possible
- [State] important matters so forcibly that the reader will be forced (or rather induced) to think out the unspoken details for himself
- [Letters] should not be flippant or frivolous,... but they may and should be good-humored, kindly, courteous
- Sincerity, honesty, is the chief source of success
- An advertisement or advertising booklets should be valuable and useful to the reader

THREE

Good Money in Good English

SHERWIN CODY'S MOVE FROM LITERATURE TO business ended up being financially profitable. It also created a legacy for him as one of the founders of modern business communication. Today, most colleges and universities teach communication courses as part of their business curriculum, and courses stress attention to customers' interests and needs. One hundred years ago, however, practical business education was just getting organized. The first university business school in the United States had begun at the University of Pennsylvania in 1881 (its Wharton School), and the earliest university courses in business communication were offered in the early 1900s—at the University of Illinois in 1902 and at New York University in 1906.[1] But relatively few people attended universities. Instead, aspiring office workers in the late 1800s typically learned about business writing from etiquette manuals, and later from books specifically designed to instruct people in letter writing.[2]

Cody's 1903 volume on *Rhetoric,* part of *The Art of Writing and Speaking the English Language,* was one of the first to stress business writing as the basis of education in rhetoric. Cody opened the book with that topic because he considered it to be of most interest to the average reader. He led with correctness, reminding readers that "First of all, a business letter should be strictly grammatical."[3] Cody suggested that a business writer should write clearly, should avoid commercial jargon, and should know the interests of the correspondent. He advocated brevity and a conversational approach rather than the style of literary English. These tenets—clarity, correctness, conciseness, and colloquial style—are still taught today, and they form the basis for such works as Joseph Epstein's *Style* and William Zinsser's *On Writing,* among many others.[4]

Cody's earliest advice on business writing was part of his larger course on English, but he quickly saw a new market. His *Success in Letter Writing* and *How to Do Business by Letter* (published in 1906 and 1908) were among the earliest stand-alone books aimed at effective business correspondence, and they developed the conversational approach more fully. Cody organized his letter-writing advice around the form of letters (salutations, closing, punctuation) and around themes such as "applying for a position," "how money is collected," and "letters to ladies." He also provided exercises, sample letters, and grammar summaries. Cody also saw letter writing as a foundation of language study and of public speaking. Written and spoken language skills were different but interconnected, Cody thought, and letter writing was not just a business skill but a model of the short essay. A good business letter was also an imaginary conversation with a reader. In *How to Do Business by Letter,* Cody wrote:

> There is a close connection between good letter writing and skill in conversation. The difference lies in the fact that the good letter writer takes part in a condensed, imaginary conversation, while the real conversationalist must usually have the stimulus of the occasion and interesting people. But the way to become a good letter writer is to practice imaginary conversation.[5]

The centrality of letter writing—not just to business but also to literacy, good English, and persuasive ability—was a recurring theme for Cody. He felt that there was no better way to practice the skills needed to hold an audience's interest. At the same time, Cody saw business writing as connected to literary studies, arguing that short story analysis and creative writing gave an advertising writer or journalist the "power of moving human nature by words."[6] Cody stuck with this theme in later works, writing in 1908 that "business letter writing is not a study of forms and usages. It is rather a study of human nature and 'how to use words so as to make people do things.'"[7] Throughout his life, Cody would return again and again to letter writing as foundational, and one of his last books, *Letters: Writing to Get People to Do Things,* began by suggesting that cheap postage had opened the entire country to business and social opportunities by mail.

Historians of business communication credit Cody and a handful of others with establishing modern business communication and popularizing the notions of clarity, correctness, courtesy, and conversational style. Cody was not the first to propose these ideas to an American business audience. That distinction probably goes to J. Willis Westlake, a professor of English at the State Normal School in Millersville, Pennsylvania, who published *How to Write Letters* in 1876.[8] Westlake emphasized that most writing was in the form of letters, and he suggested that students would be better off writing letters than literary themes. He recommended adapting one's style to the mood of the reader, and he also included special directions for typing, since that was a new technology at the time. By the early 1900s, ideas like Westlake's were clearly in the air, and various writers were assembling the components of practical rhetoric into books on business communication.

One of the others thinking about business writing in the early 1900s was George Burton Hotchkiss, a professor at the New York University School of Commerce, Accounts and Finance. Around 1909, Hotchkiss developed a 12-book series for correspondence education called *Business English* and, like Cody, he included the ideas of clarity, correctness, conciseness, and courtesy in his course.[9] Other correspondence handbooks and training courses on business letter writing were appearing as well, including one for the newly established LaSalle Extension University. LaSalle's 1911 series on *Business English* was developed by Edwin H. Lewis, a professor at the University of Chicago, who had been one of the readers of Cody's *The Art of Writing and Speaking the English Language* and who had earlier written an English textbook that included a chapter on letter writing.[10]

Cody was not writing in an era in which writers credited their influences extensively, and he was just one among many advocating a practical, colloquial model for business writing. As business historian Carter Daniel has emphasized, however, Cody was an especially influential voice in promoting the conversational tone in business communication and in the application of practical psychology to business writing.[11] His long career, high profile, broad connections, and voluminous publications gave him a preeminent voice as a business communication expert for many years. One of the ways in which Cody gained prominence was his role in education reform, and that is where we turn next.

FIGURE 3.1. The headline of an early ad for Cody's books.

SCHOOL AS BUSINESS

The first quarter of the twentieth century was a difficult one for American schools. The growth of industrialization and commerce gave business a new influence over schools, whose mission was increasingly seen as training workers. At the same time, progressive reform and muckraking journalism targeted education along with the meat-packing industry, patent medicine scams, and insurance and stock manipulation. In 1903 *The Atlantic Monthly* featured an influential article that called for schools to be run like businesses, and the language of business management soon found its way into National Education Association rhetoric and into such textbooks as William Bagley's influential *Classroom Management.*[12] Local school boards would soon begin to be dominated by business leaders.

The school reform of the early twentieth century had its roots in the efficiency movement known as Taylorism, whose intellectual leader was Frederick Winslow Taylor, a Philadelphia Quaker born in 1865. Working as an engineer in the 1880s and 1890s, Taylor studied such topics as metal cutting, the design of shovels, and the handling of pig iron, and he went on to examine work flow, time use, and incentive systems. In 1909 his influential writings were published as *Principles of Scientific Management,* and Taylor outlined five key managerial principles: science rather than intuition, harmony rather than competition, cooperation rather than individualism, maximum output, and the development of worker productivity. Taylor was something of a utopian, seeing scientific management as applying to all problems and to workers and managers alike. But while his ideas were popular with many reformers, they also came to be associated with unscrupulous cost-cutting. After Taylor's death in 1915, the idealistic side of Taylorism was often ignored, and some efficiency advocates promoted scientific management and industrial engineering as a system in which workers were easily interchangeable and replaceable.

Cody mentioned Taylor's work approvingly in his 1913 book *Business Practice Up to Date,* and Taylorism was a natural fit for Cody's image of himself as an engineer and applied scientist. He saw himself as creating similar efficiencies for business education and English teaching.[13] His criticism of schools was partly motivated by his dissatisfaction with his own education, which he saw as intellectually challenging but impractical, but Cody also had a business reason for getting involved in school reform. He had been frustrated in trying to sell schoolbooks to urban schools because of competition from larger publishers, so he may have seen a good market opportunity for textbooks and tests in a reformed, standardized school curriculum.

Cody quickly established himself as a reformer promoting ways to teach English more efficiently. Listing his affiliation as "School of English, Chicago, Ill.," he contributed an article to the first volume of the *English Journal* published by the newly established National Council of Teachers of English. Cody's "Scientific Principles in the Teaching of Composition" alluded to Taylorism and criticized traditional methods of teaching writing as overly concerned with literary models as opposed to business correspondence and advertising writing. He also criticized (without naming names) traditional textbooks as too comprehensive and unwieldy. The result was "a mental indigestion that has dissipated the intuitive mental powers of the student to an alarming degree."[14] Instead, Cody suggested a modern scientific method. He recognized that science had long been distrusted by language teachers, but thought that if teachers of composition had adopted scientific principles earlier, they would "not be spending an infinite amount of energy teaching a subject without getting proper results."[15] Cody's article also discussed the difficulty of grading compositions in crowded schools with large class sizes. He advocated correcting papers orally in class and having students write corrections as the teacher dictated them. Written criticism was better in principle, he noted, but only if students paid attention to the comments, which was "very doubtful." Since many students tended to make the same errors, it was "foolishly unscientific" not to have the whole class listen to the comments, and he outlined a system of student self-editing and peer editing.[16] Cody would be a critic of the education system throughout his career. While lauding the efforts of teachers, he was harsh about the efficiency of institutional education, and in his 1944 *Coaching Children in English,* one of his last publications, he referred to the schools as "a great social grinding machine" which only graduates half of those enrolled.[17]

THE GARY PLAN

Cody was also involved in the most famous test of the efficiency movement in American schools, the reorganization of the Gary, Indiana, school system. Located on Lake Michigan not far from Chicago, Gary was the headquarters of U.S. Steel, and the steel industry was deeply influenced by Taylor's ideas. In 1907, the Gary school system hired William Wirt as superintendent to reform its schools. Wirt was a proponent of teaching such practical and vocational skills as woodworking and pattern making, and he also saw the value in physical and social development along with the traditional three R's and academic subjects. Wirt had developed what he called the "work-study-play" model at another school in Indiana, and he introduced it in the Gary school system in 1908. The "work-study-play" model broke up the school day into discrete activities involving vocational training, academics, and recreation. It also organized school logistics around movement between homerooms and specialized rooms for music, art, geography, chemistry, and other subjects.[18] The system allowed the incorporation of new vocational activities that had previously been impossible, and it promised to make better use of school facilities. Wirt published a short explanation of the system in the *American School Board Journal* in 1911, and others began to promote the Gary system as an example of scientific management and of the elimination of waste.[19] Soon the plan was receiving public support from a number of education leaders and was even praised by John and Evelyn Dewey in their book *Schools of Tomorrow*.[20] By 1930 the system was used in over 1,000 schools, mostly in urban areas where population growth had placed new demands on school capacity. The Gary plan was not without controversy, however. When Wirt was hired as a consultant in 1915 to introduce "work-study-play" into the New York City schools, parents expressed concerns about the vocational aspects of the new method and about the effect of cost-cutting. Funding of schools and education became an issue in the 1917 New York mayoral campaign, and eventually the plans for Wirt to reorganize the New York school system fell through.[21]

As Wirt was developing his system, Cody was also studying school efficiency in Chicago. He had become interested in school and employee testing in 1912 when, as a member of the Chicago City Club's committee on education, he was asked to convene a group to study the relationship between schools and business. His committee reported a gulf of perceptions between business leaders and teachers. Cody found that business leaders believed teachers were responsible for "fundamentally bad" teaching in English and arithmetic. Teachers, in turn, saw businessmen as "vague and superficial" in their ideas about education.[22] However, Cody was certain that teachers would be willing to base their curricula on business standards if standards were less vague, and he proposed that employers themselves commit to testing the students coming out of the public schools. Such tests would represent scientifically devised standards of employment that businesses could use to determine a starting salary. Cody felt that reliable tests would be useful in hiring beginning office workers for the right job and would save millions of dollars in turnover costs. In 1915 he took the next step of founding an organization of businessmen and educators to pursue this idea. *The New York Times* described his National Associated Schools of Scientific Business as an effort to put "commercial education on a more practical and scientific basis through the adoption of definite standards." Cody was the managing director, and the committee included, among others, the then Governor of Michigan, Woodbridge N. Ferris, who had established the Ferris Industrial School in 1894.[23] The National Associated Schools of Scientific Business received some financial support from the U.S. Bureau of Education, and it worked with a variety of schools and businesses such as the National Cloak and Suit Company, the National Cash Register Company, the Burroughs Adding Machine Company, the Commonwealth Edison Company, Swift and Company, and Marshall Fields.

The business standards developed by Cody's group covered the ability to copy an address correctly and legibly, to do business arithmetic quickly and accurately (including fractions), and to correctly spell a few hundred commonly used business words. The standards also included the ability to recognize and punctuate a sentence and the ability to recognize and correct certain errors in grammar, word usage, and pronunciation. Cody next developed a series of National Ability Tests to go along with the standards. He promoted these as measuring the ability "to perform common operations in the business office" and as benchmarking "the fundamental education which all office employment presupposes."[24] Beginning in 1915, after consultation with various companies, Cody released about 20 tests based on results from 500 young office boys and girls, general clerks, stenographers, secretaries and bookkeeping clerks, and vocational students. As he developed tests and issued grading keys, Cody explored physical formats for scoring exams that would be most efficient and useful to employers. As a result, his tests and grading keys were formatted so that individual scores could be compared with the averages for various classes of employees. Cody's work also prompted him to think about grading and standards, and he distinguished between the passing standard required in subjects like Latin and Greek (60%–70%) and what was needed for business credibility (100% accuracy). Cody promoted his tests as encouraging students to work toward a 100% standard in subjects like spelling, and 100% was an ongoing catchphrase in his books and courses.[25]

Interest in validating his tests and his ideas about teaching grammar led Cody to an eventual collaboration with Wirt. In the spring of 1917, Cody piloted a grammar curriculum for about 1,000 students in both Gary and Racine, Indiana, measuring students' improvement in spelling, grammar, and punctuation. After five weeks of drill with his system, Cody found a 40%–50% reduction in the number of students' errors.[26] Under Wirt's auspices, Cody later offered the tests in New York schools as well, and by 1920 he was developing a YMCA curriculum for the teaching of *Standard Test English,* linked to the National Ability Tests.[27] Cody's experiences with Wirt and the Gary schools would be a running theme in his later correspondence course advertisements, many of which contained the subheading *What Cody Did at Gary.*

The work with the National Associated Schools of Scientific Business and in the schools had acquainted Cody with research being done on commercial and employment testing by such people as Edward L. Thorndike, Walter Dill Scott, and Frank Thompson. Cody also familiarized himself with the tests developed in 1905 by French psychologists Alfred Binet and Théodore Simon, which evolved into the Stanford-Binet tests in 1916. He researched the Point Scale of Intelligence that Robert Yerkes developed in 1915 for the U.S. Army to use in classifying soldiers for various duties. And he studied the standardized educational tests, such as the Courtis Tests in Arithmetic, being used by schools and by some employers. Cody summarized the results of these studies, his work with the National Associated Schools, and his collaboration with Wirt in a book called *Commercial Tests and How to Use Them.* The book outlined Cody's vision of the National Ability Tests as a means to raise the standards of schools "by measurement and competition and above all by the use of a single national standard."[28]

This vision was utopian. Cody saw school standards and employment tests as tools that would create a national test-based meritocracy rewarding achievement and proficiency. By providing a basis for distinctions in hiring, ability tests would end the practice of level pay for new employees and would encourage students to be more diligent. Cody predicted that "As soon as employers begin to complete for the best talents, they will pay more for the good help, and less for the poor; and where pupils are now satisfied with mere 60 or 70 per cent passing marks, they will then try to make the highest possible grades, since their ratings will make a difference in the pay at which they will be able to start to work."[29] He noted that businesses would also benefit by being better able to distinguish between those worth six, eight, or even ten dollars a week and by reducing the turnover costs that come with poor hiring. He even envisioned an Efficient Employment Register of workers that "would make it possible to control and use the available [labor] supply so as to save a waste in distribution from present haphazard methods."[30] For Cody, business education and testing were part of a broad progressive reform of the schools, which had for too long focused on a "narrow, specialized proficiency" in limited traditional subjects. "The broad power to think in a clear, businesslike way," he wrote, "is far more important and is more difficult to develop."[31]

THE MAN WHO SIMPLIFIED ENGLISH

If students were going to be tested for grammar and business ability, they would need study materials, and that was where Cody's earlier work on speaking and writing the English language came in. *The Art of Writing and Speaking the English Language* had established Cody as a practical teacher rather than a theorist. From his books on letter writing and business usage,

Cody had some experience in simplifying grammar and spelling to minimal essential points and the most common misspellings. From his private correspondence teaching and work in the schools, Cody was aware of the problems of correcting and grading student work. He was beginning to position himself as an applied scientist with a businesslike approach to subject matter and benchmarking. The natural next step for him was a correspondence course adapting the methods of testing to self-instruction. The course he envisioned would have short and simple explanations of grammatical points, supplemented with self-corrected quizzes to help students focus on individual errors. It would be an innovative use of self-instruction, aimed at providing students with passable speaking and writing skills and at preparing them for the National Ability Tests that would certify their merit. For Cody, the course was part of his utopian vision of meritocracy. It was part of his entrepreneurial vision as well, since it would position him as a provider of both the English curriculum and the English tests. In fact, the grammar, punctuation, and spelling items of the Ability Tests were often reused in the *100% Self-correcting Course in English Language,* though Cody does not make a point of this in his course. It is, however, evident from material presented in *Standard Test English* and the *100% Self-correcting Course.*

Entering middle age, Sherwin Cody was an independent scholar and a critic of schools. He had a home in the Chicago suburb of Lake Bluff, where his and Marian's circle of acquaintances included Vachel Lindsey, Edgar Lee Masters, and Margaret Anderson, all part of a summer colony of writers in the town. Marian Cody was able to travel to England periodically, and the whole family even took a year's vacation in Europe in 1911. Cody was doing well as an advertising consultant, publisher, writer, teacher, and test-maker. His School of English was located in the Chicago Opera House, and he was a member of the Chicago City Club, with connections to Midwestern politicians, educators, and business leaders. The National Business Ability Tests were showing some promise, and he had a fresh idea for a self-correcting correspondence course. Cody realized, however, that there was only so much he could do on his own, and he was ready for assistance from the emerging advertising profession in New York.

FOUR

What You Want and Where to Get It

In the final 30 years of the nineteenth century, the national wealth of the United States quadrupled. Then it doubled again by 1914.[1] Business was the new American philosophy, and advertising copywriters were its philosophers. During the 1880s and 1890s, advertising had been associated with the multimillion-dollar business in blood bitters, snake oils, catarrh pills, kidney and liver treatments, rheumatism cures, and expectorants, many of which were simply bottled liquor. Patent medicine had a straightforward advertising formula: identify a malady—real or imagined—and then sell a cure. Patent medicine manufacturers understood that they were treading on shaky ground with their products, and their great fear was state regulation. Some even included clauses in their advertising contracts voiding them if state regulatory laws came into effect, thereby applying economic pressure to the print media. Nevertheless, health-conscious magazines and muckraking journalists slowly eroded the influence of the patent medicine industry. In 1892 *The Ladies' Home Journal* stopped taking patent medicine advertising, and in 1904 it published chemical analyses of some medicines. In

October of 1905, another muckraking magazine, *Collier's Weekly,* began series of exposes of "The Great American Fraud" written by Samuel Hopkins Adams. The newly formed American Medical Association joined the attack, and in 1906 the Pure Food and Drug Act required ingredients to be identified. The end was nearing for patent medicine advertising, but not for many of the techniques that had been developed.

In the twentieth century, the advertising business was beginning to see its role as creating demand for manufactured products and consumer goods like automobiles, refrigerators, and radios as well as for food and grooming products like Wheatena, Crisco, Cutex nail polish, and Listerine. A prospectus for *McClure's Magazine* in 1904 explained this straightforwardly. It showed a young boy reading a magazine, presumably *McClure's,* and saying to his mother "Mamma, you know magazines are very useful. They tell you what you want, and where to get it."[2] The advertising business even played a role in World War I by aiding in war recruiting. As the progressive reform movement waned, skepticism about business was replaced by confidence in a continually improving standard of living. In fact, by 1925 advertising was so much a part of American life that advertising executive Bruce Barton, the son of a Congregationalist minister, would write an account of Jesus Christ's life portraying him as an entrepreneur.[3] Barton's thesis was that Christ had the qualities of a successful business leader and salesman: personal magnetism, an understanding of people, organizational ability, and sincerity. Christ himself did not endorse the ad business, but President Calvin Coolidge did, lauding it in a speech to the American Association of Advertising Agencies in 1926. Coolidge stressed that advertising had an important educational role because "It informs its readers of the existence of commodities by explaining the advantage to be derived from their use and creates for them a wider demand."[4]

Within the advertising business itself, there were different perspectives on the copywriter's role. Some agreed with Coolidge and saw themselves as professionals whose job it was to educate the public and advance society. To them, advertising was a profession just as medicine, law, and teaching were, and they were writers in a particularly challenging literary form. This professionalization even led to galleries of advertising art, prizes such as the Harvard Advertising Award, and agencies boasting of college graduates and even PhD's working for them. Other copywriters, however, saw advertising in terms of sales rather than literary merit. This group saw its role as getting results, and advertising historian Roland Marchand refers to such bottom-line copywriters as the "real pros" rather than professionals.[5]

Sherwin Cody took his idea for a correspondence course to an advertising agency made up of some of these result-oriented "real pros." The Ruthrauff & Ryan Advertising Agency specialized in mail-order sales, and Maxwell Sackheim was one of their young copywriters. In his autobiography, Sackheim wrote of meeting Cody in 1915, commenting that "Cody was difficult to listen to" because of his idiosyncratic speech. Other copywriters at Ruthrauff and Ryan were impatient with him, but Sackheim encouraged Cody to complete the correspondence course he had in mind and to patent its self-correction method. With Sackheim's help, Cody franchised his course to two Rochester, New York, businessmen, Walter R. Paterson and Charles S. Lennon, who were involved in running other correspondence schools for civil service testing. Sackheim's autobiography quotes from a letter Cody wrote to him in 1920: "I came to New York with a vague idea of an English course, and you helped me to shape it up into commercial form."[6]

Sackheim helped Cody shape the course and strategy, but his greatest contribution was in writing the first advertisement using the headline "Do You Make These Mistakes in English?" Sackheim had learned about the advertising business from Wilbur Ruthrauff, who had begun his career as a patent medicine copywriter, and Sackheim used the patent medicine formula of identifying a malady and offering a cure.[7] The malady in this case was bad English, and the cure was Cody's patented self-correction method. Sackheim's copy fit with the theme of Cody's earlier ads for his book series (such as "Good Money in Good English"), emphasizing how the product—a course in correct English—would lead to career opportunity and social advancement.

The ad led with class-conscious examples of mistakes in English and concluded its leading paragraph by noting that "Every time they talk or write" many people "show themselves lacking in the essential points of English." The implication was that if someone lacked English skills, a job that required talking, writing, and managing was harder to achieve, and if someone was known for faux pas, he or she would find it difficult to fit in to a better, more refined social group. The message targeted those who were ambitious yet uncertain.

The "Do You Make These Mistakes in English?" advertisement reflected Cody's views on salesmanship as well, which were outlined in his 1915 *How to Deal with Human Nature in Business*. There Cody wrote that "The first step in creating desire is to put yourself in the other man's shoes. Look at life from his point of view. Begin by saying 'you' not 'I.'"[8] Cody and Sackheim had the same basic approach in mind, and the "you-viewpoint" was reflected in most (but not all) of Cody's ads.

Sackheim and his friend Harry Scherman soon formed their own ad agency, and Cody's account went with them. When Sackheim and Scherman later sold their agency to Victor Schwab and Robert Beatty, Cody remained with the new Schwab & Beatty Agency, where his account was managed by Sackheim's protégé Victor Schwab. Schwab became a pioneer in direct-mail research, and he took particular pride in the Cody ad as an example of the scientific approach to advertising.[9] In an article for the industry journal *Printers' Ink Monthly*, Schwab referred to it as "An Advertisement That Is Never Changed," and he gave a ten-year comparison of responses to two different headlines, "Do

You Make These Mistakes in English?" and "How to Speak and Write Masterly English." Schwab found that the cost per inquiry and the response rate were vastly better for the ad asking speakers about their mistakes (374 ads brought 224,025 inquiries and 10,962 orders with a total value of $328,860, versus the "How to" version, for which 251 ads brought only 52,304 inquiries and 3,861 orders with a total value of $115,830).

Schwab also offered an analysis of the success of the advertisement, commenting on each of eighteen parts and seven headings or subheadings. His commentary was not particularly sophisticated, but it reveals some of the thinking that went into the copy. Schwab wrote that the ad promised "worthwhile information," it looked "painless to read," and it did not "look too much like an advertisement." Interrogatives like *why* and *what* in subheadings kept the reader interested, and the ad contained several points of proof about Cody's accomplishments. It also had some emotional appeal in its indignation about schools and traditional English instruction, and it provided a layer of academic credibility by referring to the Sherwin Cody School. The ad copy used the recurring theme of simplicity, and it opened and closed by appealing to the reader's interest in success. Finally, Schwab added that the photo of Cody had "impressive attention value" and served as a trademark of sorts, since Cody's image was by then well known and showed him to be "quite obviously an educator; dignified, impressive."[10]

Schwab especially emphasized the word selection of the headline, which contained both an appeal to the reader's insecurity and a promise to explain mistakes in English. The word *you* focused on the reader rather than the product. The modifier *these* implied specifics that would help readers to decide whether they need the product, and Schwab suggested that without *these* the headline "Do you make mistakes in English?" would imply criticism of the reader. Even the choice of the word *English,* as opposed to alternatives like *grammar, writing,* or *speaking,* was designed so that readers could connect the headline with their own weaknesses.

In its text, the typical Cody ad led off with examples of errors in English and asked why so many people are "deficient in the use of English." Subheads guided the reader along, moving from why people make mistakes to Cody's credentials, the method, results, and finally to action. The ad explained that Sherwin Cody discovered why people make mistakes by "scientific tests, which he gave thousands of times," and it assigned institutional blame to the schools. Shifting to the positive, the ad promised a course based in practice rather than rules, recounted Cody's successes in Gary to establish his credentials, and again invoked the exclusivity of a patented 100% self-correcting device.

The scientifically tested device that corrects one's bad habits was "Mr. Cody's voice behind you, ready to speak out whenever you commit an error," and the ad copy told the reader that Cody would be a patient "everlasting mentor beside you, a mentor who would not laugh at you, but who would, on the contrary, support and help you." Since Cody's patented, scientific system found your mistakes, you needed to do less work. You could make progress in just 15 minutes a day by concentrating on your weaknesses only. Finally, readers were reminded of the value of what they would gain: "a trade-mark of breeding that can not be erased." The implication was that language, more than anything else, is used to assess one's potential. By eliminating the errors associated with vulgarity and ignorance, a man or woman could pass as one bred to elegant speech.

Cody's ad appeared widely, in slicks, pulps, comics, and papers. It was a fixture of the *New York Times Book Review,* running over a hundred times. The peak years of *Times* advertising for Cody were the 1920s and 1930s, with nine ad placements in 1930 alone. By the 1940s, Cody ads were being run just three times a year, and in the 1950s just twice a year, typically in August and December as school terms were beginning. Over the years, the copywriters associated with his account experimented with a number of headlines with the hope of identifying the ones

Do You Make These Mistakes in English?

Sherwin Cody's remarkable invention has enabled more than 100,000 people to correct their mistakes in English. Only 15 minutes a day required to improve your speech and writing.

MANY persons use such expressions as "Leave them lay there" and "Mary was invited as well as myself." Still others say "between you and I" instead of "between you and me." It is astonishing how often "who" is used for "whom" and how frequently we hear such glaring mispronunciations as "for MID able," "ave NOO," and "KEW pon." Few know whether to spell certain words with one or two "c's" or "m's" or "r's" or with "ie" or "ei," and when to use commas in order to make their meaning absolutely clear. Most persons use only common words—colorless, flat, ordinary. Their speech and their letters are lifeless, monotonous, humdrum.

Why Most People Make Mistakes

What is the reason so many of us are deficient in the use of English and find our careers stunted in consequence? Why is it some cannot spell correctly and others cannot punctuate? Why do so many find themselves at a loss for words to express their meaning adequately? The reason for the deficiency is clear. Sherwin Cody discovered it in scientific tests which he gave thousands of times. *Most persons do not write or speak good English simply because they never formed the habit of doing so.*

What Cody Did at Gary

The formation of any habit comes only from constant practice. Shakespeare, you may be sure, never studied rules. No one who writes and speaks correctly thinks of *rules* when he is doing so.

"Stepping Stone To Advancement"

"The Course was a stepping stone for me. Soon after I enrolled I was promoted to Chief Clerk. Later the Course was invaluable in helping me pass the bar examinations; 67% failed. Also aided me in passing a number of Civil Service examinations." Albert F. Nebelsick, Route 2, Sunman, Indiana.

"Great Help and Benefit"

"Your Course is quite the most interesting way I have ever studied English. I feel that it will be of great help and benefit to me in my secretarial work, and to me it is money well spent." Mrs. Reba Shields, 622 Ivy St., Jacksonville, Fla.

"Money Spent Wisely"

"To anyone seeking a knowledge of English I recommend the Course most heartily. I really enjoy writing letters now, because I express myself more effectively. I can truly say that I spent my money wisely." Mrs. Martha S. Marlowe, 3030 Grade St., Chicago, Ill.

Overcomes Inferiority Complex

"It has helped me a great deal, and it has given me an added sense of security when addressing other persons. It is surprising to find how lax one becomes in the use of English, especially when one has been out of school for some years. My mind and ambition had become somewhat stagnant, and I suffered from an inferiority complex. Mr. Cody's lessons have been of great help to me in overcoming these weaknesses, for which I am thankful." Mrs. Verne Cunningham, 608 W. Emerson, Monterey Park, Calif.

Here is our mother-tongue, a language that has built up our civilization, and without which we should all still be muttering savages! Yet our schools, by wrong methods, have made it a study to be avoided—the hardest of tasks instead of the most fascinating of games! For years it has been a crying disgrace.

In that point lies the real difference between Sherwin Cody and the schools! Here is an illustration: Some years ago Mr. Cody was invited by the author of the famous Gary System of Education to teach

SHERWIN CODY

English to all upper-grade pupils in Gary, Indiana. By means of unique practice exercises *Mr. Cody secured more improvement in these pupils in five weeks than previously had been obtained by similar pupils in two years under old methods.* There was no guesswork about these results. They were proved by scientific comparisons. Amazing as this improvement was, more interesting still was the fact that the children were "wild" about the study. It was like playing a game!

The basic principle of Mr. Cody's new method is habit-forming. Anyone can learn to write and speak correctly by constantly using the correct forms. But how is one to know in each case what is correct? Mr. Cody solves this problem in a simple, unique, sensible way.

100% Self-Correcting Device

Suppose he himself were standing forever at your elbow. Every time you mispronounced or misspelled a word, every time you violated correct grammatical usage, every time you used the wrong word to express what you meant, suppose you could hear him whisper: "That is wrong, it should be thus and so." In a short time you would habitually use the correct form and the right words in speaking and writing.

If you continued to make the same mistakes over and over again, each time patiently he would tell you what was right. He would, as it were, be an everlasting mentor beside you—a mentor who would not laugh at you, but who would, on the contrary, support and help you. The 100% Self-Correcting Device does exactly this thing. It is Mr. Cody's silent voice behind you, ready to speak out whenever you commit an error. It finds your mistakes and concentrates on them. You do not need to study anything you already know. There are no rules to memorize.

Only 15 Minutes a Day

Nor is there very much to learn. In Mr. Cody's years of experimenting he brought to light some highly astonishing facts about English.

For instance, statistics show that a list of sixty-nine words (with their repetitions) *make up more than half of all our speech and letter-writing.* Obviously, if one could learn to spell, use, and pronounce these words correctly, one would go far toward eliminating incorrect spelling and pronunciation.

Similarly, Mr. Cody proved that there were no more than one dozen fundamental principles of punctuation. If we mastered these principles, there would be no bugbear of punctuation to handicap us in our writing.

Finally he discovered that twenty-five typical errors in grammar constitute nine-tenths of our everyday mistakes. When one has learned to avoid these twenty-five pitfalls, how readily one can obtain the facility of speech which denotes the person of breeding and education!

When the study of English is made so simple, it becomes clear that progress can be made in a very short time. *No more than fifteen minutes a day is required.* Fifteen minutes, not of study, but of fascinating practice! Mr. Cody's students do their work in any spare moment they can snatch. They do it riding to work or at home. They take fifteen minutes from the time usually spent in profitless reading or amusement. The results really are phenomenal.

Sherwin Cody has placed an excellent command of the English language within the grasp of everyone. Those who take advantage of his method gain something so priceless that it cannot be measured in terms of money. They gain a mark of breeding that cannot be erased as long as they live. They gain a facility in speech that marks them as educated people in whatever society they find themselves. They gain the self-confidence and self-respect which this ability inspires. As for material reward, certainly the importance of good English in the race for success cannot be overestimated. Surely, no one can advance far without it.

FREE—Book on English

It is impossible in this brief review, to give more than a suggestion of the range of subjects covered by Mr. Cody's new method and of what his practice exercises consist. But those who are interested can find a detailed description in a fascinating little book called "How You Can Master Good English in 15 Minutes a Day." This is published by the Sherwin Cody School of English in Rochester. It can be had by anyone, free upon request. There is no obligation involved in writing for it. The book is more than a prospectus. Unquestionably, it tells one of the most interesting stories about education in English ever written.

If you are interested in learning more in detail of what Sherwin Cody can do for you, send for the book "How You Can Master Good English in 15 Minutes a Day."

Merely mail the coupon, a letter or postal card for it now. No agent will call. SHERWIN CODY SCHOOL OF ENGLISH, 8811 B. & O. Building, Rochester 4, N. Y.

SHERWIN CODY SCHOOL OF ENGLISH
8811 B & O Building, Rochester 4, N. Y.

Please send me, without obligation on my part, your new free book "How You Can Master Good English in 15 Minutes a Day." No agent will call.

Name..........

Address..........

City.......... Zone No. (If any)....... State..........

☐ If 18 years or under, check here for Booklet A

FIGURE 4.1. Do you make these mistakes in English?

that generated the most replies. John Caples reported on a test run in which the reader-centered "Do You Make These Mistakes in English?" was tested against the same ad with a manufacturer-centered headline: "The Man Who Simplified English." The reader-centered headline yielded twice the results of the manufacturer-centered one.[11] Sackheim and Schwab tried other headlines and approaches as well. Sackheim used small ads in 1919 and 1920 to focus on the product with headlines like "15 Minutes a Day Gives You a Wonderful Command of Language," "A New Invention that Finds and Corrects Your Mistakes in English," and "Astonishing Facts about Your English." Schwab experimented with variations on the "Mistakes" theme, portraying speakers embarrassed in various social settings. "Do You Make These Mistakes in English?" was the gold standard, however, and Schwab often cited it in other articles he wrote on the science of copywriting. Schwab and Beatty gained both prestige and revenue from their management of the Cody campaign and even featured their work for Cody in an ad for their agency in 1956. Showing two Cody ads and reporting on split-run testing, they concluded that "Copy-testing of this kind can take much of the guesswork out of advertising," adding that "the actual response of *consumers* decides conclusively which is the better ad."[12] Cody would certainly have agreed.

Headlines over the Years

A New Invention that Finds and Corrects Your Mistakes in English

Stop Making Mistakes in Speaking and Writing!

Astonishing Facts about your English

Stop Abusing the English Language

His New Invention Finds and Corrects Your Mistakes in English

His simple invention has shown thousands how to break bad habits in English

New Way to Find and Correct Your Mistakes in English

Mistakes in Writing and Speaking Made Every Day

Your English is your trade-mark—it tells just what you are

Ten Mistakes in English—How Many Will You Make?

If only people knew how they are hurt by their unconscious mistakes in English!

His simple invention has shown thousands how to stop making embarrassing mistakes

How to Discover Your Mistakes in English in One Evening

Are YOU ever overheard making mistakes like these?

What are YOUR Mistakes in English?

Stop Groping For Words!

Sherwin Cody's New Method Has Improved the English of 41,000 People

How to Avoid Embarrassing MISTAKES In ENGLISH

Does Your English Help You or Hurt You?

He *thinks* he is speaking Correct English! Can you find his FIVE mistakes?

Which of These Mistakes in English Do You Make?

How You Can Master GOOD ENGLISH—in 15 minutes a day

FIVE

The 100% Self-correcting Course in English Language

If you clipped Cody's coupon from *Black Mask*, *Physical Culture, The Ladies' Home Journal,* or the *Chicago Tribune* and requested the free book on English, you received something called *How You Can Master Good English—in 15 Minutes a Day*. This advertising booklet expanded on the themes of *Do You Make These Mistakes in English?* Cody began with economics, citing a Carnegie Institute of Technology report that business success is due to the ability to influence others, and he asked "Do you want to get a raise—secure a new position—get ahead faster? . . . Good speech will help you avoid making a bad impression. It will provide a means of calling attention to your abilities, which may now lie dormant because your speech has not conveyed your potential to your employers."[1]

Cody's target audience was both the workplace and the social world. He asked how "a carpenter, a machinist, a factory worker" can use good English to advance, but he also gave the example of a newly rich woman at the New York opera, whose "murderous English" revealed her lack of education.[2] The anecdote cited her use of *ain't* and statements such as "Between you and I, I don't think much of them Eyetalians," as leading to social stigma. Cody linked slang, cursing, poor pronunciation, and bad grammar with a lack of breeding, and he invoked human nature to explain what happens if you don't try to improve your English. "How," he asked, "can anyone be other than critical of a person who does not seek to improve himself? . . . You cannot help it, no matter how fond you may be of him."[3]

Cody provided some brief success anecdotes—a stenographer who became the private secretary to a corporation president by improving her English and a factory supervisor who advanced to a level requiring better language skills. He described a woman seeking to join a club who misused words like *ubiquitous* and who pronounced *often* with a *t,* and he contrasted her with another woman whose home study of English led her to be mistaken for a Vassar, Smith, or Wellesley graduate even though she "never went further than one year in high school."[4] Graphics reinforced his points with images of a successful stenographer, a group of well-dressed women around a tea-service, workers reading on break, a man in a suit making a forceful point, and smiling men lined up at a cashier's window.[5]

Cody explained that the level of the course was for just about anyone. It covered "the fundamentals of the English language, English composition, and English literature from the very beginning (seventh grade of the public school, where formal study of grammar is first taken up) to entrance to Harvard, Yale or Princeton."[6] And he returned to the opening theme of economic value by comparing the cost of a college education (which he gave as $600) with the cost of the Cody course, which was on average $30. Cody ended with the question "What can you gain from this small investment?"[7] The Cody course was for those who wanted to invest in themselves.

If the 32-page prospectus won you over and you enrolled, the full course—*The Sherwin Cody 100% Self-correcting Course in English Language*—arrived in 25 weekly booklets. The booklets in turn were divided into five sections, one for each day of the workweek, and each day focused on something different. Expression was on Mondays, spelling on Tuesdays, punctuation on Wednesdays, grammar on Thursdays, and conversation and reading on Fridays. The daily lessons were tied to other reference books published by Cody: *Success in Letter Writing* was a reference for lessons in expression, *The Art of Writing and Speaking the English Language* and his *Brief Fundamentals* provided background on punctuation and grammar, and the Nutshell Library supplemented conversation and reading.

The basic plan of the course was for students to focus on individual weaknesses. This entailed an assessment component—a self-test—and so lessons 1 and 25 included timed tests of what students knew before beginning the course and what they knew at the end. A form letter from 1924 explained the rationale:

> Who ever heard of beginning a course of study with an examination instead of a lot of rules and definitions? The reason is this: Your object is to correct your unconscious bad habits of spelling, punctuation and grammar. But what bad habits have you? You don't know. Every one else has taught English by the analytic-reasoning method, but Mr. Cody first makes you conscious of what mistakes you unconsciously make.... Mr. Cody does not want you to waste time on that which you are unconsciously doing right, nor does he want you to take a chance—he wants you to know what your weak points are and concentrate exclusively on them.[8]

This method was a natural outgrowth of business testing and the philosophy of advertising. A good English course, like a good advertisement or business letter, should serve the needs of the customer. The best way to do this, in Cody's view, was by individual instruction, and the most efficient form of individual instruction was guided self-assessment and self-correction. Cody also understood the importance of providing students with a rationale for what they were learning. His course attempted this by selecting issues of spelling, pronunciation, grammar, and word usage that were most commonly troublesome, and Cody emphasized how his system avoided the old models of comprehensive memorization of grammatical rules. And of course he linked communication to practical life goals such as sales, advertising, and letter writing.

The main vehicle for Cody's views on writing and speech were the Monday lessons on expression. These took up the first two pages of each weekly booklet, and typically consisted of an essay on some topic about writing or speaking (essentially a one-page letter to the reader) followed by a page of Cody's running autobiography. The Monday lessons gave advice on style, clarity, brevity, emphasis, imagery, and emotional appeal, and Cody included essays on conversation, news writing, story writing, and copywriting as well. The lessons also touched on broader topics of practical communication, such as the importance of good manners, humor, empathy, and audience, and they even described how to overcome self-consciousness. The autobiographical essays allowed Cody to both infuse the course with some of his personality and provided a way to introduce his ideas about education and culture. Cody explained that education should be practical and functional, but also intellectually fulfilling, and the final two biographical entries stressed Cody's dream of "a new literary art" that would bridge the cultural divide between "intellectual esthetes" and "ordinary humanity."[9] We shall return to this dream in more detail in Chapter Seven.

Monday Is for Telling Your Life Story

Most of the Monday lessons on Expression in the *100% Self-correcting Course* are a running account of Cody's life up to his fiftieth year. While the autobiography was tangential to the course, Cody explained it in term of helping readers to write their own life stories. The chapter titles below give a roadmap to Cody's philosophy and image of himself.

1. "Telling one's own Life Story" (Lesson 2)
2. "My Earliest Recollections—the Storms and Fires in Nebraska" (Lesson 3)
3. "My Father and I" (Lesson 4)
4. "The Early Education of a Country Boy" (Lesson 5)
5. "My Mother Becomes my Guardian Angel" (Lesson 6)
6. "I set out at Eleven to Earn my Living and get an Education" (Lesson 7)
7. "A Year Among the Beautiful Hills of New Hampshire" (Lesson 8)
8. "A Schoolboy's Triumph" (Lesson 9)
9. "Financial Problems of Working one's Way Through School" (Lesson 11)
10. "Starvation to Affluence in College" (Lesson 12)
11. "How I Learned to Write" (Lesson 13)
12. "What is the Value of a College Course?" (Lesson 14)
13. "The Enchanting World of Art" (Lesson 15)
14. "The Heaven and Hell of Love" (Lesson 16)
15. "Leading the Life of a Writer" (Lesson 17)
16. "Transition from Literature to Business" (Lesson 19)
17. "Psychology of Literature and Business Writing the Same" (Lesson 20)
18. "Advertising and Education at Bottom the Same" (Lesson 21)

(continued)

19. "Learning the Italian Language" (Lesson 22)
20. "Principles of Psychology" (Lesson 23)
21. "A Dream of a New Literary Art" (Lesson 24)

There were no autobiography entries in Lessons 1, 10, 18, or 25.

SPEAKING AND SPELLING

The practical lessons relied on various techniques—fill in the blank, choice among two forms, and even actual composition. The constant was Cody's avoidance of theory, definitions, and lists of rules to memorize. The Tuesday lessons began with the difference between vowels and consonants and an explanation of the syllable. Cody's definitions are understandable but not linguistically sophisticated: vowels are "the real sound letters" and consonants are sounds "which merely modify the vowels." The syllable, in turn, is "one vowel sound with consonants that can be pronounced with it."[10] Years earlier, in the *Word Study* volume of *The Art of Writing and Speaking the English Language,* Cody gave somewhat fuller definitions. Vowels were described as "full and open tones from the vocal cords made with the mouth open, and capable of being prolonged indefinitely," and consonants were described as "modifications of these open sounds, which are pronounced with or without the help of the voice, and incapable of being prolonged."[11] Later, in *The New Art of Writing and Speaking the English Language,* Cody added that "The very simple, even primitive, phonetic system" he gave was intended for "the practical purpose of an easy introduction to reading pronunciations from the Webster diacritical marks."[12]

In the *100% Self-correcting Course,* Cody discussed vowel length and diphthongs (*oi* and *ow*) and provided exercises identifying long and short vowels. He commented on variation in vowel sounds, such as the varieties of *a* (an "Italian" *ah* as in *father* and a broad *aw* as in *all*) and the weakening of vowels before *r*. At times Cody's discussion was hampered by his imperfect understanding of phonetic terminology. For example, he used the labels "hard" and "soft" to refer to two unrelated distinctions—the different pronunciations of *th* and the different pronunciations of *c* and *g*. In the first case, "hard" and "soft" *th* refer to the phonetic distinction between voiced and voiceless (as in *bathe* versus *bath*). In the second, hard and soft refer to the fricative *s* versus the stop *k* and to the affricate *j* versus the stop *g*.

Cody's penchant for simplification was also evident in the pronunciation and spelling rules he gave. He identified just two pronunciation principles as worth everyone's attention. The first was that vowels are naturally short, unless made long. Lengthening occurs by adding "silent e after the single following consonant" (for example, *sit* versus *site*), by placing an "accent on the naked vowel," or because vowels "were long in the original word from which a given word is derived."[13] His second principle was that the pronunciation of *c* or *g* is soft before *e* and *i*, and hard elsewhere (which encapsulates the contrast between the first letters of *city* and *gem* as opposed to *cape* and *game*).[14] In lesson 5, Cody added two spelling rules built on these principles. The first was that "Silent e is dropped when a syllable beginning with a vowel is added, unless required to keep c or g soft." Thus *knowledge* + *able* is spelled *knowledgeable* rather than *knowledgable*. The second rule was for doubling consonants in words such as *barred, fretting, preferred, occurrence,* and *beginning:*

> In words of one syllable, and words of more than one syllable accented on the last syllable, ending in a single consonant preceded by a single vowel, the final consonant is doubled when a suffix beginning with a vowel is added; but if the accent changes to another syllable after the suffix is added, the consonant is not doubled.[15]

According to this, *fretting* and *barred* have doubled consonants because they are derived from monosyllabic *fret* and *bar. Prefer, occur,* and *begin* will show doubling in *prefErred, occUrrence,* and *begInning* because the stress is on the second syllable. And when stress shifts, as in the case of *prEference,* doubling does not occur.

Aside from pronunciation and spelling rules, the recurring feature of the Tuesday lessons was practice in spelling. Cody's method was to give sentences with select words in a phonetic spelling and have students write the standard spelling in a blank next to the prompt.[16] The transcription was not without its curiosities: *Masachusetz* was transcribed with a final *z* rather than *s* and the examples *abreviate* and *akomodate* included a final *e* letter which of course is silent.

Some of Cody's Spelling Exercises

Do not *abreviate* your words. __________

I can *akomodate* you with a loan. __________

He made *aknolejment* of the receipt. __________

It pays to *advertīz*. __________

At the end of the first spelling test, Cody gave benchmarks: the average grammar school graduate missed nine items out of twenty-five and the average high school graduate missed six. Experienced stenographers missed only four and the best spellers just one.

Spelling lessons tended to focus on irregular words, which Cody adapted from an earlier study of 542 troublesome spelling words identified by the statistician Leonard P. Ayres. Cody also emphasized that his system of learning spelling from transcription was for adults rather than children, remarking that "While young children should never look at phonetic or wrong spelling, this will not harm adults if the correct form is always near at hand." He did not discuss word formation (what linguists call morphology) in either the *Self-correcting Course* or in *Word Study,* though he noted in the latter book that the study of prefixes helps spelling, and he gave a list of words organized by suffixes (including *able, ible, ent, ence, ant, ance, cous, ious, cious, ize,* and *ise*).

CAN YOU SPELL THESE?

The words below are from Cody's spelling exercises (without the sentence context). How many can you get? (Answers on page 54.)

curn't	*stashunery*	*didunt*
mis'lān'us	*duznt*	*mish'uneries*
en'velop	*ārōplānz*	*envel'op*
katar'	*for'ud*	*champān'*
chōfer'	*pēcūlyer*	*chŏkolat*
pincherz	*kōkane'*	*spagĕt'i*
spinaj	*awxĭl'yery*	*complumentery*
osilātz	*mēzlz*	*bĕnufish'ery*
negroz	*preseed*	*bookā*

Difficult pronunciations were also a theme of the Tuesday lessons because they could so easily mark someone as provincial or unsophisticated. Cody gave the pronunciation of a number of foreign words and names such as *attaché, ballet, beau monde, blasé, Boulanger, bourgeois, canaille, chic, cognac,* and *coup d'état.* Cody also treated English names and words that might be mispronounced because of their spelling, noting, for example, that *Concord* should be pronounced *cong kerd,* not *con-cŏrd* and that *blackguard* is *blag gard* not *black-guard.* He warned against pronouncing *devil* and *evil* with the last syllable as *ill,* against pronouncing *iron* as *ī'ron* and *England* as *eng-land* (preferring *ing gland*). He indicated a length distinction between *there* and *their,* as *thar* and *thār,* and between *shone* and *shown,* as *shon* and *shōn.*[17] Cody also included some comments on the general character of American speech as well, suggesting a tendency for Americans "to pronounce all their syllables with great exactness." He cautioned therefore that "The largest number of mispronunciations comes from trying to enunciate obscure vowels accurately, as *or* at the end of *honor, favor, error,* where properly the sound is simply that of *er.*"[18] He stressed as well the need for people to deal with personal idiosyncrasies, and he identified his own: *hor'izon* rather than *ho rī' zon, cŭl' in ary* rather than *cū' lin ary,* and *flas cid* rather than *flac(k) cid.*[19]

ANSWERS TO CAN YOU SPELL THESE?

current, stationery, didn't, miscellaneous, doesn't, missionaries, envelope, aeroplane, envelop, catarrh, forehead, champagne, chauffeur, peculiar, chocolate, pincers, cocaine, spaghetti, spinach, auxiliary, complimentary, oscillate, measles, beneficiary, Negroes, precede, bouquet

Some pronunciations and spellings have changed since Cody's time.

Cody's discussion of pronunciation showed that he understood it as both relative and informed by local standards. When authorities disagree, Cody wrote, students should "follow the prevailing fashion" of their region "if that fashion is recognized either as first or second choice."[20] For Cody, pronunciation did not need to be uniform and was best when it was colloquial: a speaker should avoid uneducated pronunciations but should also "not make himself conspicuous by adopting a pronunciation that those he associates with will consider pedantic."[21] He cautioned, for example, that the pronunciation of *ask, command, last,* and similar words with *ah* was an affectation. Implied in Cody's advice is the understanding that speakers ought to meet the expectations of their audience, along with an understanding of the public as neither unrefined nor over-refined.

WEDNESDAY: PUNCTUATION

Wednesdays dealt with punctuation: capitals, apostrophes, colons, semicolons, and even parentheses and dashes—which Cody cautioned against overusing.[22] The apostrophe was treated, with Cody preferring *James's* and *Dickens's* over *James'* and *Dickens'* because "these names are singular."[23] Hyphenation of compound words was covered as well, and Cody noted that compounds evolve from being two words to being hyphenated, and finally to being one word. Among other spellings, he recommended *anybody, any one, ball-bearing, bedroom, by-product, engine-room, facsimile, foolscap, gas stove, good-bye, vice president, under-estimate, over-confident, pin-money, pocket-knife, school teacher, schoolgirl,* and *stock-market.*[24]

The main focus in punctuation, however, was on the comma, which was "nine-tenths of punctuation."[25] He gave comma rules for compound sentences, for subordinate clauses, for modifiers, for serial words and phrases, and for dates, addresses, and quotes, along with several exercises in which commercial contexts were used, such as formatting a purchase order or punctuating a business letter. Cody's punctuation exercises did require some knowledge of grammatical terminology on the reader's part. One explanation, for example, gave the rule of thumb that "When subordinate clauses are so essential to the meaning that leaving them out would spoil the sense, they should never be set off by commas."[26] To make sense of the rule, readers must already understand the idea of a subordinate clause, figure it out from the examples given, or refer to Cody's supplementary materials.

Often, Cody organized the exercises to give practice in identifying the basic categories of grammar necessary to apply

Subordinate Clauses

Cody's exercise asked readers to "Decide which clauses in the following are to be set off by commas and which not, inserting also periods and capital letters." Readers were also instructed to mark simple subjects, predicates, subordinate conjunctions, and relative pronouns. How well can you do on this paragraph?

> Yesterday we went for a picnic to the woods which we visited last summer even before the sun was up Harold and Ellen were out of bed and getting dressed as I had packed our lunch basket the night before we had only to dress and get our breakfast I told mother that I would not let the boys go in swimming and Ellen promised to see that the girls did not take off their shoes mother was afraid that snakes might bite their feet

Answers on page 190

punctuation rules. Some comma exercises, for example, asked readers to circle or underline simple subjects and predicates, conjunctions, and prepositional phrases. As much as possible, however, Cody avoided terminology in the *100% Self-correcting Course.* When discussing restrictive and non-restrictive clauses, for example, Cody avoided those terms, noting only that "The comma has the effect of shading the meaning. You will see, therefore, that so far as absolute correctness is concerned it may be just as exact to put in a comma or to leave it out. The real difference is that you get more intelligent meaning out of words in one case than in the other."[27] Cody's example was this:

> Postal cards, which are furnished by the government, cost one cent each or two cents for a double or reply card. Post cards, which are privately printed, must bear the word "Post Card" on the address side and come within a specified size.

The commas were needed, he explained, because postal cards and post cards are different things and "the relative clauses following them merely explain the differences which already exist in the words." Cody succeeded in identifying the use of the comma without actually explaining it, and his method was often inductive in this way—teaching punctuation by examples rather than rules.

The avoidance of grammatical terminology reflected more than Cody's commitment to simplification. Cody thought that punctuation was more often a matter of experience with language than something reducible to rule. In *The New Art of Writing and Speaking the English Language,* he made this explicit by distinguishing between punctuation rules—matters of correctness—and principles of composition, such as "The comma is used to throw emphasis on what follows" or "The comma is used to suggest a contrast or change of structure."[28] Cody advised students to drill just a few rules. Instead, he thought, they should develop "instinct and observation for the refinement and exceptions" by reading and writing.[29]

In some of the supplementary material Cody offered additional interesting perspectives on publication. In *Brief Fundamentals,* for example, he described the semicolon as "a superior comma" and he distinguished among commas, dashes, and parentheses for "words thrown into a sentence for additional explanation." The various marks are used when the connection of the words to the main material was close (commas), less close (dashes), and slight (parentheses). And Cody discussed the use of quotation marks, including the quotes around slang terms, which he explained as attempts to communicate that "I have heard these words used, but I do not venture to take any responsibility for them myself."[30]

Cody's advertisement and prospectus and the Monday, Tuesday, and Wednesday lessons illuminate several key ideas of his approach to speaking, writing, and communication: simplification, self-checking, the social role of grammar, and the relativity of correctness. Cody believed that the subject matter of correct speaking

The SHERWIN CODY

100% Self-Correcting
Course in
English Language

Lesson 1

Monday: *Expression*
Tuesday: *Spelling*
Wednesday: *Punctuation*
Thursday: *Grammar*
Friday: *Conversation*
& Reading

Pat. Oct. 15, 1918
Copyright 1919-21
by Sherwin Cody

The Sherwin Cody School of English, Rochester, N.Y.

FIGURE 5.1. The patented self-correcting course.

Thursday

Grammatical Correctness

Lesson 1—Test

The practical question that arises in business on grammar is, "Is this right, or is that?" The following test puts this question in simple form. Ten principles are covered, in the ten different paragraphs: if you get one sentence in a paragraph right and another wrong, it shows clearly that you do not understand the principle—you will get half of them right by chance any way. There are 32 points in all, and even selected college graduates average one mistake. In the sixth paragraph there is a dash between pairs of sentences, one of which should be marked out.

Grammar Test

(Time, 10 minutes.)

X
1 2

Correct the following with pen on this sheet, crossing out the wrong form when two are given:

1. Every one of those men (has his—have their) pickax; Each point (is—are) as clear as a star; The woman or the tiger (come—comes) out; Montgomery Ward & Co. (have—has) settled the strike; The Montgomery Ward Company (have—has) settled the strike.

2. The ship (sank—sunk). The bird has (broke—broken) its wing.

3. He has (laid—lain) it down; When he came in he (set—sat) down; I saw that the book (lay—laid) on the table; At eight o'clock I (laid—lay) down; At eight o'clock I (set—sat) down.

4. The doctor said that fever (produces—produced) thirst; It had happened before I (saw—had seen) him; From what I saw of him he appeared (to be—to have been) a man of letters.

5. I wish Anna (was—were) here; If Anna (was—were) here, she would nurse him; If Anna (was—were) there, she was the life of the company.

6. While sitting on my doorstep, a beautiful butterfly caught my eye—While sitting on my doorstep, I caught sight of a beautiful butterfly; By doing so you will clear up the matter—By doing so the matter will be cleared up; On weighing the sugar a shortage was found—On weighing the sugar he found a shortage.

7. I saw (him—his) doing it; I approve (him—his) doing it; What do you think of (me—my) going to town?

8. I was frightened at that examination's length—the length of that examination; For (goodness'—goodness's—goodness) sake; He spoke of the land's fertility—the fertility of the land.

9. I do not like (those—that) sort of people; I belong to (that—those) kind myself.

10. He feels (bad—badly) about it; It looks (good—well) to me; The general stood (firm—firmly).

Total Errors

Grammar school graduates will average ....13 mistakes
High school graduates will average .... 8 mistakes
Experienced stenographers will average .... 5 mistakes

After having marked out the wrong word in each sentence, compare with the key and check each error in the first blank column. A week later, mark the second copy of the test and check the errors as before. Then compare your second record with your first to see if you made the same old mistakes again. Concentrate on these till you have mastered them to the 100% point.

FIGURE 5.2. Grammar Self-Test from Lesson One (answers on page 191).

and writing could be scientifically simplified, so that progress could be made in just a few minutes a day, and he believed that individual errors could be identified and eliminated by motivated self-testing, using his patented worksheets. Cody also maintained that correctness was a social passport enabling speakers to make the good impressions that permitted other strengths to be seen. This idea—a selling point really—is most strongly articulated in the ads and prospectus. In the course, Cody also acknowledged the more complicated point that correctness in language is relative. Standards fluctuate, and in order to use language well, it is necessary to develop a feel for pronunciation, punctuation, and grammar through reading, conversation, and study. Cody's course contains a fifth key idea as well—that a connection to good literature will provide both an understanding of human nature and a broad view of the world necessary for a full life. We will return to this idea in Chapter Seven, after we conclude our survey of Cody's grammatical and vocabulary lessons.

SIX

Grammar and Vocabulary

THURSDAYS WERE FOR GRAMMAR, AND HERE CODY shifted away from principles of composition to focus on norms of grammar. As usual, the first lesson was a timed self-diagnostic. The Lesson 1 self-test, which appears on the previous page, covered ten points of usage: agreement, verb forms, modification, pronouns, and the use of articles, adjectives, and adverbs. It was a chance for students to assess their understanding of traditional grammar, and Cody noted the benchmarks he had established. Grammar school graduates averaged 13 errors out of the 32 possible answers, high school graduates averaged 8 errors, experienced stenographers 5 errors, and "even selected college graduates average one mistake."[1]

What points of grammar were tested? It was impossible to be comprehensive, so Cody chose about ten grammatical concepts and gave several items for each so that students had more than one opportunity to check each concept. He tested common verb form errors by asking readers to select the correct form in examples like *The bird has (broke—broken) its wing*. He also checked less obvious verb agreement, like the agreement of verbs to subjects quantified by *each* and *every,* verb agreement to conjoined subjects like *The woman or the tiger,* and verb agreement to corporate entities like *Montgomery Ward*. Cody also tested understanding of other kinds of agreement, such as that of articles with nouns (*that kind—those kind*), and that of verbs between clauses, such as *It had happened before I (saw—had seen) him.* And he checked understanding of subjunctive forms, asking readers to select between *was* and *were* in counterfactual conditionals, such as *If Anna (was—were) here, she would nurse him.*

Cody included examples of misplaced modification as well. Students were asked to select between *While sitting on my doorstep, a beautiful butterfly caught my eye* and *While sitting on my doorstep, I caught sight of a beautiful butterfly.* The self-test included the distinction between adverb and adjective forms such as *He feels (bad—badly) about it,* and Cody tested some esoteric points of possessive usage, such as the distinction between objective and possessive case with gerunds, as in *What do you think of (me—my) going to town?* and apostrophe use in the phrase *for (goodness'—goodness's—goodness) sake.*

With a self-assessment as background, students began the grammar lessons in the second week of lessons. Cody's method was often simply to note troublesome forms, such as singular nouns ending in *-s* (*politics, athletics, tidings, nuptials, ethics*) or Latin plurals (*phenomena, curricula, alumnae*). Among other things, he focused on the forms of verbs like *awake, drink, ring, sink, shrink, sing, spring,* and *swim,* which he saw as difficult for many speakers, and he gave exercises distinguishing the often confused verb forms *except* and *accept, lie* and *lay, sit* and *set, let* and *leave, rise* and *raise, flown* and *flew, loose* and *lose,* and *may* and *can.*

Cody's approach to grammar was sometimes prescriptive and sometimes not. In the lesson dealing with pronouns, for example, he advocated the generic masculine as the correct choice for reference to nouns modified by *each, any,* and *every.* Exercises included *Every gentleman and lady left (his—~~their~~) wrap in the anteroom* and *Has anybody in the room dropped (~~their~~—his) pocketbook?* On the other hand, the note associated with *Whom will the paper be read by?* viewed the use of *whom* as awkward and pedantic, and

Cody suggested avoiding it by saying *By whom will the paper be read?* or *Who is it the paper will be read by?*[2] It is unclear why Cody did not opt for the simple *Who will the paper be read by?* Perhaps he was attempting to finesse the grammatical case of the pronoun by constructing the example with *who* as a predicate nominative rather than as the object of the preposition *by*. In *The New Art of Writing and Speaking the English Language,* Cody dismissed two other prescriptive mainstays as well, the "myth that the infinitive should not be 'split'" and the rule about not ending a sentence with a preposition, which "seems to have lasted far beyond its period of usefulness."[3]

His treatment of the pronoun *none* is another example of his flexibility. Cody warned against being misled by the etymology of *none* (as derived from *no one*), and in Lesson 8 he gave 25 examples illustrating its variability between singular and plural, including *None of the men of our day (speaks—~~speak~~) so clearly as Wilson* and *None of the Fifth Regiment (were—~~was~~) wounded.* Cody explained his reasoning in *The New Art of Writing and Speaking the English Language,* saying that "In the past some critics have contended that *none* is always singular, since it is evidently derived by a contraction of *no one,* but the best writers treat *none* as either singular or plural according as the writer is thinking of the last person or the last group of persons."[4] Overall, Cody recommended American colloquial usage to the extent that he deemed it respectable and reputable, and Cody's choices are similar to those of his contemporary Henry Watson Fowler, the author of *A Dictionary of Modern English Usage*. Regarding *none,* Fowler agreed that "it is a mistake to suppose that the pronoun is singular and must at all costs be followed by singular verbs," citing the *Oxford English Dictionary* as authority. And concerning *who* and *whom,* Fowler too noted the common colloquial use of objective case *who.*[5]

Cody was, however, often dismissive of stigmatized forms, remarking that "'Ain't' is never a proper word to use."[6] He was prescriptive as well in his discussion of the possessive, advocating its use for only for verbal nouns and for animate possessors.[7] He gave the hoary prescriptive rules for *will* and *shall,* writing that "In ordinary statements of fact in future time, use *shall* after *I* and *we, will* after other subjects. ... But if there is determination of an exercise of will, reverse the ordinary usage, and say I or we *will,* you he, etc. *shall.*" Cody tempered this with a nod to usage for *should* and *would,* telling students to follow the same rules as for *shall* and *will,* "but observe that *would* after *I* and *we* is commoner than *will.*"[8]

Sometimes descriptive and sometimes prescriptive, Cody was above all a practical grammarian who offered his readers what he thought they needed to know to avoid stigma, but he also encouraged them not to find fault in the speech of others. Cody advised that it was sometimes better to be ungrammatical than rigidly proper: "Language exists for ideas," he said in Lesson 23, "not ideas for language." The study of grammar is mainly to avoid the "catastrophe" when the effect of language is lost because the reader stops to criticize usage, grammar, or spelling.[9] Though Cody's grammatical exposition and advice was often normative, he consistently emphasized that "'authority' in grammar is an old-fashioned and very poor appeal to as compared with reason," and he tried to balance the reality of language change with the social expectation of following norms.[10]

Cody provided just a bare treatment of grammar in the *100% Self-correcting Course.* He gave a more systematic exposition in *The Art of Writing & Speaking the English Language* and other works, where he explained sentence diagramming, defined the parts of speech, and even discussed the nominative absolute (as in *He knowing that, I had no choice but to act as I did*). In the *100% Self-correcting Course,* Cody's grammatical recommendations sometimes differ from today's usage, since both the colloquial standard and prescriptive sensibilities have evolved. For example, Cody's choice of *oftener* in *You must report to me (oftener—~~more often~~)* would be awkward usage today. And certain present-day grammatical shibboleths were undiscovered in Cody's time. There is no mention, for example, of the pseudo-problem of *hopefully* as a sentence adverb, which took hold in print in the 1950s and elicited a strong reaction from conservative grammarians in the 1960s. In Cody's day, it was not an issue.

While Cody advocated flexibility in grammar, a weakness of his course was that he made no changes in his grammatical work as he updated and republished his course. There is evidence of his evolving grammatical understanding in the supplementary books, such as *The New Art of Writing and Speaking the English Language,* but the course changed so little over the years that one reviewer in 1940 dismissed Cody's grammar advice as "sometimes debatable as to its correctness, and too frequently out of date in its rulings."[11] What lessons does Cody's approach have for today's English teacher? The lesson is perhaps more in the method than in the grammatical advice. At the elementary, middle, and high school levels teachers face an environment of widespread reliance on standards and standardized testing. Their students are expected to recognize and use correct grammar, and their state curriculum standards may dictate grammar skills to be learned at each grade level, sometimes labeled as proofreading or editing skills. Like Cody, modern English teachers often begin by assessing what students know about grammar. They may try to tease out students' knowledge of grammar terminology, their knowledge of grammar concepts, and their ability to recognize and correct different types of errors. Of the three tasks, recognizing and correcting errors is thought to have the most practical importance, just as in Cody's time.

The teaching of English has moved closer to some of the views that Cody outlined in his work and away from the mere exposition of traditional grammar as a school subject. University researchers in education and linguistics have investigated what effect grammar teaching had on writing, and a 1963 review of the literature in composition even claimed that teaching grammar as a separate subject was ineffective and took time away from other language arts activities. Later studies, such as those of Robert Connors, Andrea Lunsford, and Maxine Hairston, classified the types of errors that student writers make as well as the responses of teachers and business professionals. Such work has helped to provide an empirical basis to our understanding of what errors are socially significant.[12] Teacher educators in turn have used this research to be more selective in the application of grammar to the curriculum. Educational linguist Rei Noguchi, for example, argues for grammar instruction to "be made more cost-efficient than it is now" and suggests beginning with just a few basic concepts like sentence, nonsentence, subject, verb, and modifier. And teacher educator Constance Weaver has advocated that a minimal grammar focusing on punctuation, fragments, and readability probably only requires about a dozen grammatical terms.[13] Such proposals are the natural heirs of the approach that Cody pioneered—simplifying grammar to its manageable essentials.

While grammar and linguistics remain crucial for English teacher education, teachers today tend not to rely on prescriptive or descriptive grammar, but rather tailor grammar instruction to the needs of students and integrate it into the context of writing and literature. There is still much professional discussion concerning how much and what kind of grammar to teach, but many teachers opt for grammar instruction that is informed by the role of teachers as researchers, by knowledge of the sort of errors that beginning writers make, and by activity-based approaches to classroom grammar. A good test for a bit of grammatical knowledge is to ask what problems of exposition that knowledge will solve. This too is in the spirit of the approach Cody suggested in his *English Journal* articles and in *Coaching Children to English*. In *Coaching Children,* he wrote that the best high school teachers organized grammar around activities such as "editing and publishing school papers, putting on plays, organizing and conducting various kinds of clubs," and he advocated teaching grammar in the context of literacy practice for elementary education.[14] While his grammatical advice is outdated, the general tenor of his approach seems to have held up well today.

What Are Your Mistakes in Grammar?

Try your hand at these grammar items from Cody's Lesson 8.

1. The Company (has—have) issued its financial statement.
2. Our factory (have—has) established new rules for employees.
3. The United States Army in France (have—has) fought well.
4. An army of laboring men (was—were) pouring over the bridge.
5. A few of the men (was—were) running.
6. A number of the men (was—were) running.
7. The number of men on the list (were—was) fifty.
8. A fixed number of men (is—are) drawn each year.
9. None of the men of our day (speaks—speak) so clearly as Wilson.
10. None of the Fifth Regiment (were—was) wounded.
11. The Jones Brothers Tea Company (has—have) joined the society.
12. Jones Brothers (has—have) joined the society.
13. Tait & Co. (have—has) joined the society.
14. Lloyd George's Cabinet (have—has) decided to resign.
15. Mamie Brown, together with six other girls and five boys, (have—has) appeared for examination.
16. Each of the sixteen companies of infantry and three companies of artillery (is—are) now on parade.
17. Several of the sixteen companies of infantry and three companies of artillery (is—are) on parade.

(continued)

18. Every one of the forty seventh-grade boys and the A division of girls (was—were) promoted.
19. The President's staff, including Major-General Wood, Colonel Lansing, and Major Downing, (are—is) leading the procession.
20. The first essential in choosing your studies (is—are) definite aims.
21. Captain Jones, as well as the sailors, (has—have) been wounded.
22. None of these fifty men (are—is) eligible.
23. Our class of ninety-five (has—have) just graduated.
24. The congregation of the Episcopal church (are—is) voting for a pastor.
25. The United States (are—is) demanding reciprocity.

Answers on page 192

BUILDING A BETTER VOCABULARY

Friday's lessons focused on both vocabulary and reading. We will discuss Cody's advice on how and what to read in the next chapter, and close this one with his advice on vocabulary building. Each Friday, Cody gave students a list of difficult words or word pairs and had them compose sentences using the words. Definitions and examples were given in an answer key on the following page, which allowed students to check their efforts immediately. This sentence-composition work let students practice distinctions such as those between *affect* and *effect, accept* and *except, compliment* and *complement, among* and *between, ability* and *capacity, pupil* and *student, continual* and *continuous,* and *avenge* and *revenge.* Some of the vocabulary work also dealt with preposition choice (for example, whether *die with, die from,* or *die of* was correct). It also exercised the use of the singular/plural pairs *data/datum, curriculum/curricula,* and *genus/genera* and explained the different meanings associated with alternate plural forms such as *dice/dies, fish/fishes, staffs/staves,* and *alumni/alumnae.*[15] Cody added some sentence-rewriting exercises in Lessons 19–24, presenting awkward sentences to be reworded. For instance, Cody gave students an opportunity to rewrite the sentences, "I am trying to get one of my suits on 5,000 men's backs" and "Say friend, send your drug order to Brisley's. No one has ever lived to regret it."[16]

In order to explain vocabulary distinctions, Cody distinguished among different levels of usage just as a dictionary does. He identified certain usages as old-style (*proven*) or obsolete (*disremember*) and others as Americanisms (*depot, railroad, real, smart*). Certain words were identified as vulgar (*got married*) or colloquial (*lots*). And, going a step beyond what might be found in a dictionary, he even identified some words as pretentious (*reside*). Many of the distinctions that Cody included were familiar ones from other nineteenth-century dictionaries of usage.[17] And as with grammar, some of his distinctions illustrate ways that usage has changed in the last century. Discussing *recipe* and *receipt,* for example, Cody remarked that "The preferred usage is *recipe* for a drug mixture and *receipt* for cooking." Today, of course, a recipe is a set of instruction for anything (*a recipe for disaster,* for example) and a receipt is a written acknowledgement. Cody also wrote that *claim* applies to property rather than assertions: "I may claim a piece of property, but I should not claim that this or that is true." Today *claim* is commonly used to mean "assert," so perhaps ideas have become metaphorical real estate. The usage examples in the Friday lessons also give insight into Cody's understanding of semantics and the social attitudes of his time. Like some nineteenth-century usage critics, Cody believed that vocabulary should be organized on a principle of "one form, one meaning" and that different words should have different meanings or uses. In talking about *love* and *like,* for example, Cody opted for strictness of sense by asserting that "we love people, but like pie." And he distinguished the words *lunch* and *luncheon* by level, writing that the latter is used by "ladies in society" and the former by "common folk." For the semantically similar words *person* and *party,* Cody made the one form–one meaning principle explicit, saying that "it is contrary to the principles of languages to admit a new word without some added meaning." At times, too, some of Cody's social attitudes were evident in the usage notes. Writing about the distinction between *man* and *gentleman,* he said that: "The English call a laborer a 'man,' and an aristocrat who is just as boorish a 'gentleman'; but Americans prefer to reserve the word 'gentleman' for the man who has natural instructs of high breeding." And Cody also dismissed the *-ess* ending, remarking that "*Authoress* is considered vulgar. Women who write prefer simply to be called simply authors."[18] Cody's comment also recognizes a role for the preferences of the referents of a term in deciding usage, a principle that is evident today in the guidelines of many press organizations.

As was the case with grammar and punctuation, Cody relied on a blend of illustration and explanation. For *elder* versus *older* he said merely: "He was older than I, but I call him my elder brother," leaving readers to infer the principle behind the distinction.[19] Describing a more abstract term like *science,* however, Cody was expansive. He described science as "systematized knowledge," writing that "to be a true science it must be knowledge rather than philosophy or art, and it must be thoroughly systematized. . . . 'Scientific butter-making' is straining a point in the effort to indicate that the methods of butter-making are more exactly systematized than usual."[20] Perhaps Cody's description of his own work as scientifically tested should be read in this light: the applied science of language teaching involved a thorough system of instruction systematized to identify common problem areas and to allow precise measurements of improvement.

In the Friday lessons, Cody treats an occasional point of grammar, but his usage work is primarily aimed at introducing practical distinctions that would give students a correct, conversational way of speaking. At times, however, Cody's selection of material was more esoteric than practical, as was the case in Lesson 6, where he rewarded his students with a wonderful digression listing collective nouns: *a bevy of girls, pack of wolves, gang of thieves, host of angels, shoal of porpoises, herd of cattle or buffalo, troop of children, covey of partridges, galaxy of beauties, horde of ruffians, heap of rubbish, drove of oxen, mob of blackguards, school of whales, congregation of worshippers, corps of engineers, band of robbers, swarm of locusts, crowd of people,* and *flock of birds.* Even a meat-and-potatoes practical grammar requires some dessert.

Which Is It?

Cody shared his preferences for usage distinctions with his readers. How do you use these words?

affects or effects	aggravates or irritates
an historical or a historical	at or in a small city
apt or likely	continuous or continually
awful or awfully	beside or besides
bring or carry	between or among
die of or die from	divers or diverse
each other or one another	farther or further
forward or forwards	man or gentleman
guess or think	can't hardly or can hardly
got or gotten	saleslady or saleswoman
lit or lighted	luncheon or lunch
née or né	had only or only had
pair or pairs	pants or trousers
permit or allow	party or person
reared or raised	proposal or proposition
practical or practicable	pupils or students
seem or appear	standpoint or point of view
toward or towards	to joyfully recall or joyfully to recall
unbeknownst or unbeknown	entire or whole

Cody's answers on page 194

SEVEN

The Finishing Touches

SHERWIN CODY'S *100% SELF-CORRECTING COURSE* offered more than spelling, pronunciation, punctuation, grammar, and vocabulary.[1] In the Friday lessons on Conversation and Reading, Cody included essays on English literature along with the vocabulary-building work. These literary essays advised his students on who and what to read, and they were intended to create an understanding of literary culture—what counted as well-written English prose that Cody's students might benefit from reading. Explaining the connection between literature and vocabulary, Cody suggested that reading good literature provided examples of words in context and was thus more useful than exercises aimed solely at developing a large vocabulary. Cody remarked that "It isn't more words that people want, but more ways of using them. If more words were used, common people would not understand them."[2] The way to gain real freedom in the use of words, according to Cody, was by reading well-written books, particularly fiction. And, he pointed out, a knowledge of literature also served conversation by providing people with something engaging to talk about.

The Friday essays on literature were also an opportunity for Cody to promote his Nutshell Library series. First published in

1907, each Nutshell volume presented an evening's reading on a particular author along with excerpts and abridgements intended to give readers a taste of that writer's best work. Readers of the Nutshell volumes could then decide for themselves what they wished to read more fully. The Nutshell Library included Robert Burns, Sir Walter Scott, Charles Lamb, Henry Wadsworth Longfellow, Nathaniel Hawthorne, Charles Dickens, Alfred Tennyson, William Shakespeare, Washington Irving, William Makepeace Thackeray, and Abraham Lincoln.[3] Like all of Cody's work, the Nutshell volumes aimed at efficiency and self-direction. Cody explained: "The best way to get interested in great literature is to take one author at a time, learn something about him as a man of letters, and read a little now and then at odd moments from his finest work.... If you read too much at one time, you may get sick of him before you know him."[4] The volume on Shakespeare, to take one example, gave a few pages of information on Shakespeare's life and then abridged *The Merchant of Venice, Romeo and Juliet,* and *Hamlet.* Most of the other books followed this pattern, though the volume on Lincoln, the one nonliterary figure included, was primarily biography. The Lincoln volume included the First Inaugural Address, the Emancipation Proclamation, and the Gettysburg Address, as well as a selection of Lincoln's anecdotes. Cody seemed to be especially taken with Lincoln's prose, which he endorsed in the *100% Self-correcting Course,* as "The style admired and used in American business, in advertising, in salesmanship, at the bar, and in the pulpit when the highest effects are produced."[5]

The initial volume in the Nutshell series, titled *How to Read and What to Read,* was different from all the others. It was Cody's survey of literature, covering poetry, fiction, and essay writing in "an attempt to separate the dead wood from the living."[6] In *How to Read and What to Read,* Cody discussed what made good poems, essays, and novels, and he picked landmarks of modern literature. The volume was also Cody's treatise on the study of literature, connecting literature to psychology and to the intellectual, ethical, and aesthetic aspects of life. Literature should be uplifting rather than merely representational, Cody felt, and it should do more than provide depictions of "our lives of toil."[7] Cody saw literature as motivational and aspirational. It should, he said, "give us ourselves idealized and in a dream, all we wished to be but could not be, all we hoped for but missed." Cody also saw books as serving a broader audience than the literary elite, remarking that the authors in the Nutshell Library "are not called Masters because they appeal to 'highbrows,' but because their work is so great that it moves and stirs vast masses of people, millions of men and women like you and me."[8]

He also emphasized that if businessmen were going to lead successful and well-rounded lives, more was needed than practical communication skills. He reminded readers that life had a practical side in which a living was made and a personal side which had to do with self-understanding. Reading good literature, Cody said, teaches us to live "as a part of the larger sphere of being." But even as he advocated the larger sphere of being, Cody recognized the limits of many literary works, writing that "Great classics of the past are dead for us if they do not connect up with our present thought and emotion."[9]

While it may be tempting to gloss over Cody's discussions of literature as filler or even conceit given the largely practical orientation of his course, Cody's literary lessons fall in the American tradition of self-education through books. In the nineteenth century, Ralph Waldo Emerson was arguing for reading as a means to self-reliance, self-knowledge, and self-trust—autonomy in the intellectual sense. In his essay on "Books," Emerson presented general rules about what to read along with an annotated list of the best reading. Influenced by Emerson, others developed their own recommendations. Yale University president Noah Porter's *Books and Reading: What Books Shall I Read and How Shall I Read Them,* published in 1870, contained advice on fiction, nonfiction, and religious reading, including a 40-page list of recommended books prepared by James Hubbart of the Boston Public Library.[10] And in Chapter Nine, we will look at Charles W. Eliot's Harvard Classics, which were a particularly salient influence for Cody.

For many, the pursuit of literature was associated with a search for inward truth, and one's character was both shaped and demonstrated by books owned, read, or aspired to. In the Gilded Age, American writers sometimes de-emphasized the connection of book culture to wealth, even presenting the two as being at odds.[11] Cody's approach was of this tradition and apart from it. Like Emerson, Cody stressed literature as a means of personal growth, but he did not see humanistic values as opposed to materialistic ones. Rather, he also saw literature as complementing an interest in the commercial world—as a way in which a businessman could engage in personal study for intellectual and moral development. Cody dismissed the attitude of many aesthetes about materialism and commerce. In the biographical entry in Lesson 24, he recalled his rejection by literary friends when he turned to business:

> According to the literary code of those days, I was a renegade from art, and my friends in London disowned and condemned me privately. Business was to them anathema, and I had adopted the ideals of the philistines. But more and more, I felt that they were wrong; and that advertising with its motto "Truth" and salesmanship with its motto "Service," in short American business, were phases of a high game as daring, as noble in its possibilities as the chivalry of the Middle Ages.[12]

It is no accident that Cody ends his course with these sentiments. He saw the promotion of a new literary art as one of his life goals and thought that the Great War had created an audience ready for literature that catered neither to the "low ideals of a merely amusing fiction" nor to the tastes of "exclusive aristocratic individuals who despise . . . the vulgar, swaying crowd of ordinary humanity."[13] Middle-class book culture did in fact expand after World War I, and it also became increasingly guided by experts. The *New York Herald Tribune*'s Books section, edited by Stuart Sherman, was begun in 1924 and treated books as a form of news.[14] John Erskine initiated Columbia University's Great Books seminar in 1920 and promoted engagement with canonical writers both in academe and among the general public, through popular articles and volumes like *The Delight of Great Books*. And the Book-of-the-Month Club used a panel of literary judges led by Yale professor Henry Canby, who selected each month's noteworthy books, balancing the goal of educating and uplifting the public with the practical issue of maintaining strong sales.[15]

Cody's literary recommendations, like Stuart Sherman's, John Erskine's, and Henry Canby's, bridged tradition and modernism. The Nutshell Library itself was clearly rooted in the nineteenth century, but Cody's four-page list of recommended books in *How to Read and What to Read* would eventually include such modern writers as Erskine Caldwell, Sherwood Anderson, Sir Arthur Conan Doyle, Theodore Dreiser, William Faulkner, Ernest Hemingway, James Joyce, Sinclair Lewis, Somerset Maugham, Thomas Mann, Booth Tarkington, and Thornton Wilder. Cody's recommendations also included many works by women, including Pearl Buck, Willa Cather, Dorothy Canfield Fisher, and Ellen Glasgow.[16] Another indication of the changing market of literature was in the final chapter of *How to Read and What to Read*. In his 1937 edition, Cody replaced an earlier discussion of children's literature with one about modern fiction, noting that the twentieth century brought about an era of sexual frankness, "a complete banishment of sentimental pretense," and a focus on "social ambitions and realistic life."[17] Society and literature were changing, and the adult market for books was becoming as significant as the school market.

Finally, Cody's approach to literature also reflected his ambivalence about the education he had received. As Christopher Newfield has emphasized, apart from the cosmopolitan East Coast it was not widely evident why young people would want to attend college or what practical benefits they would receive from doing so.[18] Dissatisfaction with the impracticality of higher education was widespread in the nineteenth century, and as a result the classical tradition was giving way to a more practical education. As this shift occurred, the literary humanities were no longer the primary means of creating a disciplined, educated person. Increasingly, the humanities were seen as finishing touches to an otherwise practical education. Cody's literary lessons fall in the middle of this shift. His own tastes were formed in the nineteenth century, shaped by his studies at Amherst and his period as a reviewer, biographer, and aspiring novelist, and he disdained cheap fiction and the popular press. But his focus on the market and on practicality led him to see the older canon as something to be approached selectively. Cody never used the term *middlebrow,* but his literary selections were aimed at "the average man who reads the newspaper more than he ought, and would like to know the really interesting books in standard literature which he might take pleasure from and which might be of some practical benefit to him."[19] Just as his advice on language embraced the colloquial while acknowledging the prescriptive tradition, his advice on reading sought to find that which was useful in the tradition and to discard the deadwood.

EIGHT

Every Day People Judge You

Cody's 25-week course aimed at teaching the practical norms of speaking and writing, encouraging a flexible, businesslike approach to grammar and an understanding of human nature through literature. His advertisements tended to stress only the first of these, getting customers' attention with the promise of a patented shortcut to linguistic success, social acceptance, and the appearance of breeding. Cody's advertising strategy was not alone in this approach, and in fact reflects broader advertising themes common in the 1920s and 1930s. Historian Roland Marchand has studied that period and has identified several recurring themes of text and imagery, which he calls parables. Two of the parables identified by Marchand are especially evident in Cody's ads: the parable of the first impression and the parable of the democracy of goods. In addition, Cody's advertising emphasized a third important theme not in Marchand's typology, the ethic of advancement through self-study. Consumers' response to these narratives was essential to the success of Cody's course and to other correspondence education as well.

We begin with first impressions. The parable of the first impression was simply the idea that the impression we make lays the groundwork for future interactions and success. Anxiety about social judgment was used to sell dental care products, chewing gum, bath soap, shaving cream, razors, and house paint. An early ad for Listerine mouthwash, for example, showed a couple dancing and asked "How's Your Breath Today?" An advertisement for Cutex nail polish had the caption that "Every Day People Judge You by your Nails," explaining that "just a few minutes' care once or twice a week" would result in nails that are "a decided addition to your personal charm."[1] It was not just social acquaintances who made judgments based on first impressions. Advertising campaigns were built on the idea that the first impression you make with managers determined your success or failure in the workplace:

> The parable of the First Impression, for all its exaggerated dramatics, drew much of its persuasive power from its grounding in readers' perceptions of contemporary realities. In a relatively mobile society, where business organizations loomed ever larger and people dealt far more often with strangers, many personal interactions were fleeting and unlikely to be repeated. In large organizations, hiring and promotion decisions now often seemed arbitrary and impersonal.[2]

Many workers assumed that personnel decisions were made by a managerial group with more refined tastes and values, and so appearances and impressions could make all the difference. In order to get a chance, you needed to both know your job and be clean, fresh-smelling, and well-spoken. And of course you needed to stay that way.

The selling of first impressions was in some ways an extension of a long-standing American concern for correct behavior. Etiquette books and conduct books had been common since colonial times, and historian Arthur M. Schlesinger, Sr., has noted that works like Ben Franklin's *Autobiography,* Eleazar Moody's *The School of Good Manners,* and Henry Peacham's *The Compleat Gentleman* were very popular among affluent colonials. Such books defined correct behavior in terms of respectfulness, modesty, and piety.[3] At the same time, there was another view of etiquette that held that "good breeding was founded not upon considerations for others, as the moralists taught, but upon consideration for self."[4] The most influential early example separating ethics from morals was Chesterfield's *Principles of Politeness*. This work emerged from the advice of Philip Dormer Stanhope, 4th Earl of Chesterfield, to his illegitimate son. Published first as letters to his son in 1774, the book contained exhaustive advice about how to impress, influence, and manipulate others. In various edited and expurgated forms, Chesterfield's book became popular in the nineteenth century as a book of manners and behavior, and it was even published in special American editions.

As Schlesinger emphasizes, changing social and economic conditions nudged etiquette in America away from character and toward behavior. The expansion of the nation, the rise of the common man, and the social divisions between New England and the South all fostered attention to outward manifestations of behavior. Post–Civil War etiquette books recognized etiquette as arbitrary convention, often dealing with such topics as facial hair, tobacco, the use of calling cards, how long to keep callers waiting, and when to use a knife, fork, or spoon. During the twentieth century, mass production of body care products and the influence of advertising strengthened the link between appearance and etiquette, and a positive first impression came to be seen as a way of not offending others. First-impression dangers could be corrected by products like mouthwash, razors, and nail polish. They could also be managed by avoiding social and linguistics offenses, and products like Cody's *100% Self-correcting Course* were part of the same consumer consciousness as soap and deodorant.

Marchand identified another important narrative theme in the advertising of the 1920s—one that he called the parable of the democracy of goods. The democracy of goods refers to the way that a rising standard of living, mass production, and mass distribution placed goods that were once prohibitively expensive within reach. It meant, as Marchand writes, that everyone could "enjoy society's most significant pleasure, convenience, or benefit."[5] Automobiles, washing machines, and better homes were all possible, and advertisers stressed that what was once only for the wealthy was now available to, and even expected of, the middle class. One indication of the new attitude was introduction of the phrase "Keeping Up with the Joneses," taken from Arthur "Pop" Momand's comic strip, which debuted in 1913 and featured the never-shown Joneses as a perpetual object of envy.

It wasn't just durable goods that were more widely available. Ideas and information once available only to millionaires now seemed within the reach of the middle class as well. Applied science and psychology were making education, training, and work more efficient, and the distribution of information was becoming more efficient and democratic as well. Mass production of books made knowledge available to readers, and inexpensive magazines and cheap postage provided ways to learn about the books you needed to keep up with the Joneses. Marchand talks about the democracy of goods, but it may be just as important to consider the democracy of information that was made possible by mass production and media.

Cody's advertisements were part of the democratization of information. They did not have the look of many of the slick magazine ads of the 1920s. Rather, the ads were intended for easy reproduction in pulp magazine and newspaper formats, so they are light on graphics and heavy on text.[6] But Cody's campaign stressed first impressions as relentlessly as any slick magazine campaign for razors, soap, or life insurance did. His ads reminded working and middle-class readers that, fairly or unfairly, they would be judged by their speech and writing. And the references to Cody's "Wonderful New Invention," his patented scientific method, and the mere 15 minutes required invoked democracy and availability every bit as much as ads for washing machines in the slick magazines.

The narratives of the democracy of goods and of first impressions had staying power in the 1930s, as the Great Depression led to more hard-edged advertising. When a rising standard of living could no longer be marketed, the focus shifted instead to holding onto your job and preserving economic security for your dependents. The Prudential Insurance Company, for example, had featured ads in the 1920s explaining that "life insurance provides a way to give old age the comforts and consideration it so richly deserves." In the 1930s, Prudential explained instead that "Many a lapsed policy has deprived a child of full-time schooling" and warned that "The Life Insurance Policy that would have saved their home was permitted to lapse."[7] Even ads for razors and pajamas focused on jobs: a Gillette razor advertisement from the 1930s, for example, illustrated the impact of a five o'clock shadow on the ability to get a job, as a dejected husband explains that "I didn't get the job." And an ad for Duofold Health Underwear led with the question "SICK—will you hold that job?"[8] Cody's ad, with its appeal to first impressions and to the democracy of goods, did well in both the ambitious 1920s and in the desperate 1930s.

Cody's ads also featured a third narrative theme, not highlighted by Marchand. This is the narrative of self-improvement, a theme that overlaps with first impressions but is distinct from it. Cody's ads, like ads for other books and courses, stressed the long-standing American belief in self-study. Workers of the 1920s and 1930s were being introduced to the idea that practical learning was a lifelong commitment. By the 1920s, the 30-year-old International Correspondence Schools offered technical and business courses that ranged from accounting to wool manufacturing. ICS, as it became known, advertised itself cozily as "The University of the Night" in an ad which showed a man lying on the floor before a fire, contentedly studying at home.[9] But it also relied more directly on the idea that success was due to self-study. One ad, for example, showed a husband handing money to his wife and saying, "Here's an Extra $50, Grace—I'm Making *Real* Money Now."

FIGURE 8.1. An ICS "warning" ad.

The ad copy celebrates the success of the couple due to his study and her encouragement:

> Yes, I've been keeping it a secret until pay day came. I've been awarded a promotion with an increase of $50 a month. And the first extra money is yours. Just a little reward for urging me to study at home. . . . We're starting up easy street, Grace, thanks to you and the I.C.S.![10]

Another ad took the opposite approach, implying that failure to take an ICS course would mean being left behind. A manager tells a downcast employee:[11]

> We just can't take any chances about promotions these days. We must select a man on his ability to do the job, not on the basis of his ability to make friends. I know you've been here for a long time, but you know that you have never made any effort to acquire training that would fit you for the jobs ahead. The men I promote have been utilizing their spare time.

A first impression counted, but so did continual self-improvement. Ads like these blended the promise of financial rewards, the fear of missing out on promotions, and the ease of studying at home.

These three themes allowed advertisers to shape a powerful message to American men and women in the 1920s and 1930s. It was an uncertain world, in which a bad impression or grammar error could do lasting damage. But knowledge was available to everyone, even those with limited time and money. All that was needed was the determination and character to study on your own. The total effect was a persuasive case to readers that anyone could get ahead, and keep up, if they wisely used products to improve their skills and manage the impressions they made.

NINE

Just 15 Minutes a Day

SELF-IMPROVEMENT WAS NOT JUST FOR GETTING ahead at work. Some products also focused on the presumed elite knowledge and the depth of intellect that arose from serious books. Yet, as we shall see, impression management and the democracy of goods were themes in these efforts as well. Reading was a good thing in itself, but it could be done in an efficient, egalitarian way and could help an average industrious person attain the cultivation and gravitas of the very well-read.

A good place to begin is with Charles W. Eliot, the education reformer and long-time president of Harvard University who lent his university's name to the series of books known as the Harvard Classics. Eliot was himself a Harvard graduate and taught there for a time before embarking on a brief business career and then accepting a professorship at the nearby Massachusetts Institute of Technology. He was tapped to be the president of Harvard in 1869 at the young age of 35. Eliot served more than 40 years as Harvard's president, advocating practical education, science, modernization of the humanities, and an elective system that tried to fit education to the individual. Eliot became something of a celebrity public intellectual whose opinions were sought after and seriously considered, and he was a frequent commentator on academic and public policy issues such as admissions quotas, football, imperialism, women's rights, racial equality, and prohibition.

As biographer Hugh Hawkins emphasizes, Eliot had been impressed with the growth of correspondence schools and Chautauqua reading circles, and his speeches often stressed the importance of continuing education through reading good books.[1] He often claimed that, for the right person, a five-foot-long shelf of great books could substitute for the liberal education a college provided. In 1909, near the end of Eliot's presidency, editors at Collier Publishing approached him with the idea of developing a library of such books. Eliot obtained permission to use the Harvard brand, and his assistants identified a set of readings in history, philosophy, religion, education, science, politics, literature, and the fine arts.[2] The choices included some of the dialogues of Plato (the *Apology,* the *Crito,* and the *Phaedo*), the *Odyssey,* the *Aeneid,* the *Divine Comedy,* Augustine's *Confessions,* works by Charles Darwin (*The Origin of Species* and *The Voyage of the Beagle*) and John Stuart Mill (*On Liberty* and Mill's *Autobiography*), four plays by Shakespeare, Ben Franklin's *Autobiography,* and *The Thousand and One Nights.*[3] The Harvard Classics were in the tradition of expert advice about reading and books that included Emerson's essay on "Books" as well as Noah Porter's *Books and Reading*. Eliot's crimson-bound Harvard Classics, however, went beyond previous reading guides, however, by providing excerpts from the books rather than just advice for home reading. Just as Cody saw his Nutshell Library as encouraging an interest in great writers, Eliot had in mind a sampling of thought that would encourage further reading.

Of course, when the idea of the Harvard Classics was announced, Eliot's celebrity status and the academic suspense of what would be selected gave the project some public interest and cachet. Eliot no doubt saw the Harvard Classics as an opportunity to further serve the public as he entered the final phases of his long career. The trustees of Harvard must have also seen an opportunity to spread the university's influence and name, but others questioned the handing over of the Harvard brand to a commercial publisher like Collier. As Hawkins notes, John Jay Chapman, a Harvard graduate from 1884 and a critic of the Harvard Classics, wrote disapprovingly about the replacement of intellectual values with business values and about the use of the Harvard name in advertising.

One of Chapman's critiques was that once the project was underway, control would be ceded to Collier.[4] Nowhere was the handling over of control more evident than in the advertising campaign for the Harvard Classics. Early ads focused on the contrast with classical education ("No more Latin, no more Greek, no more sittin' on a hardwood seat") and the enjoyment of reading ("If you are a lover of books"), and some ads traded on Eliot's fame. Soon, however, Collier's ads invoked the democracy of goods, self-improvement, and the importance of first impressions. "Why treat your mind like a merry-go-round" by indiscriminately reading, one ad asked. Since Eliot had approved the choices of what to read, elite education was available to all, just like other mass-produced goods. Later ads stressed efficiency in other ways, noting that the low price and easy terms meant that "It May Never Again Be So Easy to Own the Famous Harvard Classics." Still other ads made direct appeals to financial success, with headlines such like "What 15 Minutes a Day Has Done to My Husband's Earning Power." And some touched on psychology and class consciousness with the headlines "How to Get Rid of an INFERIORITY COMPLEX" and "Why Envy Them Longer?"[5]

Efficiency, first impressions, and self-improvement were stressed in the ad copy. The Harvard Classics were presented as a way to improve one's mind, with readers reminded that "In all of the world there are only a really few works that have *made history,*" and that "To read *these* few great works systematically and intelligently is to be really well read." The Classics were efficient as well, and Collier emphasized that Eliot's reading system was used by 100,000 businessmen because it "shows how to select a library without waste or worry, what books are *worth while* and what are not."[6] The free prospectus booklet, the *Fifteen Minutes a Day Reading Guide,* reiterated these themes, emphasizing the desire to appreciate the best that the world had to offer:

> But now, what of *your* mental life, your growth in vision and power? Do you spend *your* precious reading time with the daily paper or the book that happens to come your way? It all depends, in the last analysis, on your ambition. If you are satisfied with yourself, with your business and social position, with your mental equipment—well and good. But if you want for yourself *the best* that this eventful and fascinating world has to offer, you simply cannot afford to overlook these stepping stones to achievement that have been laid for you.[7]

The prospectus opened by reminding readers of the importance of books "in the matter of making a life as well as a living." And it emphasized that while the Harvard Classics entertained, they also served a higher goal of mental growth. "The day of the untutored success is passing," it was noted.[8] Being well read was necessary for success, popularity, and confidence. The prospectus appealed to the character of readers and their desires for an efficient road to success, but it also directly addressed first impressions. The page headed "15 Minutes a Day Makes All the Difference" made it clear that acquiring a "rich mental background" can make the difference between being someone who is "listened to eagerly" and being someone who has little to say. Like Sherwin Cody's *100% Self-correcting Course,* the *Harvard Classics* drew on anxieties at the same time that it stressed success through efficient self-education. Eliot dealt with all the liberal arts and Cody just practical English, but each tried to distill the tools for personal growth, social success, and financial advancement to just 15 minutes of effort a day.

15 Minutes a Day Makes All the Difference

Here are two men, equally good-looking, equally well dressed. You see such men at every social gathering. One of them can talk of nothing beyond the mere day's news. The other brings to every subject a wealth of side-light and illustration that makes him listened to eagerly.

He talks like a man who has traveled widely, though his only travels are a business man's trips. He knows something of history and biography, of the work of great scientists, and the writings of philosophers, poets, and dramatists.

Busy as he is with the affairs of every day, he has found time to acquire a rich mental background.

To-day a quarter of a million men and women who appreciate the distinction that belongs to the cultivated, well-read person are attaining it in contact with the great books in the Five-Foot Shelf, under the guidance of Dr. Eliot.

FIGURE 9.1. From the Harvard Classics prospectus.

"I HAVE BEEN TOLD THAT YOU ARE A BOOK-LOVER"

The *100% Self-correcting Course* and the Harvard Classics illustrate book culture as an important consumer trend of the early twentieth century. And if those modern consumers were not enamored of the traditional works excerpted in the Harvard Classics or Nutshell Library, there was soon an alternative. In the 1920s the Book-of-the-Month Club began to sell contemporary books by mail, offering readers books that were serious but not academic.

The club was born out of an earlier venture called The Little Leather Library, which had been the idea of booksellers Charles and Albert Boni and two ad writers, Harry Scherman and Cody's friend Maxwell Sackheim.[9] They had seen the market for the classics evident in Eliot's success, and in 1915 borrowed money to publish 2,000 sets of 30 titles. With advance orders from the Whitman Candy Company, the Little Leather Library Corporation began by producing small leather-bound editions of Shakespeare included as premiums with candy and soon moved on to department store and direct mail sales. The list of titles expanded to about 100, but according to Sackheim, by the mid-1920s, the market was saturated, so Sackheim and Scherman thought of a new way to market books by subscription. In 1926, together with a businessman named Robert Haas, they came up with a plan to capitalize on the public thirst for books. Scherman and Sackheim knew from experience that it was difficult to sell single books, and so they created a mail-order club to promote repeat business. There were some problems at first. The original Book-of-the-Month Club sent books to members without any advance notification, allowing people to return the book if they didn't care for it. Returns were a costly problem, however, and Sackheim suggested providing notification to readers that a certain book would be sent to them unless they returned a form. The advance notification approach—known as the negative option—gave the

Book-of-the-Month Club a healthy profit, and the Club prospered independently for over seventy years.[10]

The success of the Book-of-the-Month Club was in part due to unique marketing and distribution, but it was also due to the role of books as symbols. Books and written language represented education, and owning books was a form of impression management, creating a social display of intellect, class, and income. Expensive-looking books, cultural historian Janice Radway has emphasized, showed that a family "placed a high premium on education, tradition, beauty, and taste."[11] As copywriters, Sackheim and Scherman understood this instinctively. Their direct mail appeal for the Little Leather Library began: "You don't know me from Adam, but I have been told that you are a book-lover, that you have bought good books in the past, and that apparently you like to have them around you."[12] The inaugural advertisement for the Book-of-the-Month Club emphasized even more directly the reader's need to be included in the world of books:

> How often have outstanding books appeared, widely discussed and widely recommended books you were really anxious to read and fully intended to read when you "got around to it," but which nevertheless you missed! Why is it you disappoint yourself so frequently in this way?[13]

Like Cody's and Eliot's advertisements, this Book-of-the-Month Club ad identified a problem—too many books in too little time—and it offered an efficient solution in its product. Though they were selling books and education, not blood bitters and liver pills, the *100% Self-correcting Course,* the Book-of-the-Month Club, and the Harvard Classics relied on the advertising techniques of the patent medicine tradition: disease and cure. This simple technique was effective because the consumer consciousness of the time stressed self-improvement, first impressions, and the democratization of goods. The result of this mix of old ideas about self-improvement together with new ideas that arose from social and industrial change was a robust market for self-study books and courses. It was a market that encompassed both the working class, through projects like the International Correspondence Schools, and the middle class, through the Harvard Classics and the Book-of-the-Month Club. And Cody's course, which advertised in both the *New York Times Book Review* and adventure magazines like *Black Mask,* aimed at both audiences.

TEN

A Better Self: Manners, Music, and Muscles

The Harvard Classics, the Book-of-the-Month Club, and the *100% Self-correcting Course* reflect the centrality of literature and language to early twentieth-century self-improvement culture. But there were other ways to invest in yourself as well. The physical culture movement, for example, focused on exercise, strength, diet, health, and even sex. Another market niche existed in teaching special skills that would impress others. And there was always an interest in learning how to behave properly. From the 1920s through the 1940s, etiquette, music, foreign languages, physical strength, self-confidence, and much more were sold in advertising campaigns for special books and courses. These advertising campaigns provide a further picture of the ways in which anxiety and desire marketed self-improvement in the early part of the twentieth century, and the ways in which self-improvement was changing as well.

Etiquette is a good beginning, since books on correct behavior have always been popular in America. As noted earlier, etiquette was an evolving concept throughout the nineteenth century. Conduct books for rural life gave way to books of manners, and the focus of such books shifted from traits of character to traits of behavior. The twentieth century also required a thoroughly modern notion of social correctness. People lived in different locales and at different paces, they grew more affluent and expectant, the roles of women began to change, and World War I and Prohibition tested the limits of behavior. All of these things helped to push aside many Victorian conventions and created the market for a new series of etiquette books for the new century.[1]

The most famous of these was Emily Post's *Etiquette, The Blue Book of Social Usage,* published in 1922.[2] A year earlier, however, a woman named Lillian Eichler penned *The Book of Etiquette* for the Nelson Doubleday publishing company. Eichler was a young advertising copywriter at Ruthrauff & Ryan, and she had written the ad copy for an older etiquette book by Doubleday. While her ad was remarkably successful, the book itself had a high return rate, so Doubleday commissioned Eichler to write a modern etiquette manual that would stay sold. Eichler took on the commission and wrote the *Book of Etiquette* and its ads.[3]

While ads like Cody's and Eliot's addressed the reader directly to explain the benefits of the product, Eichler's ad, like many others of this era, used stories to suggest how people's lives would be changed by the product. Her most famous work was one titled "Again She Orders—A Chicken Salad Please." In this ad, a young woman disappoints her date and herself by repeatedly ordering the same meal when they dine out. The unnamed protagonist's life is limited because she is unfamiliar with the French items on the menu and with the proper utensils for restaurant dining, so again and again she orders a chicken salad. Another *Book of Etiquette* ad, titled "Both are Embarrassed—Yet Both Could Be at Ease," explained:

> Every day in our contact with men and women little problems of conduct arise which the well-bred person knows how to solve. In the restaurant, at the hotel, on the train, at a dance—everywhere,

> every hour, little problems present themselves. Shall olives be taken with a fork or the fingers? What shall the porter be tipped, how shall the woman register at the hotel, how shall a gentleman ask for a dance—countless questions of good conduct that reveal good manners.[4]

Eichler drew on insecurities about everyday social situations. She reminded readers that there is no discomfort worse than not knowing what to say and do at all times, and her ads keenly captured the social anxiety of twentieth-century etiquette. One series of ads chronicled the misadventures of Violet and Ted Creighton, a fictitious couple whose manners cost them dearly. In one, they are having dinner with Ted's boss. After several embarrassing faux pas by Violet and Ted, the boss takes Ted aside to tell him that "I'm sorry Creighton, but I decided to consider Roberts for the vacancy. I need a man whose social position is assured."[5]

Eichler's ads treated etiquette as the finishing touches to social conduct and as a route to social advancement. Her book itself took a somewhat more nuanced view. Explaining the role of manners in society, *The Book of Etiquette* explained that modern etiquette involved respecting the conventions of society concerning "one's appearance, manner, and speech," but that it also involved tolerance, "carefully disciplined impulses," and "regard for the rights of others."[6] While etiquette defined in this way still had an association with character, it was increasingly defined in terms of the first impressions created by appearance and manner. This is clear in Eichler's discussion of language as an aspect of etiquette. In volume two of *The Book of Etiquette,* she devoted consecutive chapters to Speech and Dress. The chapter on Speech began by emphasizing that "One is judged by his dress but this judgment is not final. A better index is his speech. It is said that one can tell during a conversation that lasts not longer than a summer shower whether or not a man is cultivated." The same sentiment is found in Cody's ads, which described correct language as offering "a trade-mark of breeding."[7]

Other mail-order possibilities went beyond the avoidance of social gaffes to the idea of becoming more popular and admired. The U.S. School of Music, founded in 1898, offered correspondence instruction in voice and speech, singing, and instruments as diverse as the piano and the ukulele. A classic 1926 advertisement by Ruthrauff & Ryan copywriter John Caples characterized musical ability in terms of the admiration of one's friends. Titled "They Laughed When I Sat down to Play the Piano," the ad began with a narrative: "Arthur had just finished playing 'The Rosary.' The room rang with applause. I decided that this would be a dramatic moment for me to make my debut." To the amazement of his friends, the narrator (Jack) played a difficult piece by Franz Liszt. When asked how he had learned to play, Jack responded he had never seen his teacher and a while ago couldn't play at all:

> Then I told them the whole story. "Have you ever heard of the U.S. School of Music?" I asked. A few of my friends nodded. "That's a correspondence school, isn't?" they exclaimed. "Exactly," I replied, "they have a new simplified method that can teach you to play any instrument by note in just a few months."[8]

The ad explained the benefits of the U.S. School of Music method: its simplified teaching method allowed progress in just a few minutes of study each day and at a cost of just a few cents a day. It required "no laborious scales" and no teacher. If readers were unsure whether they had any musical aptitude, they could send for a free booklet which provided a Musical Ability Test, and if they lacked musical instruments, those could be provided as well. "They Laughed When I Sat Down to Play the Piano" appealed more to the desire to impress than to fear of embarrassment, and the approach worked so well that Caples repeated it in other ads, including one for the French-at-Sight course which led with the headline "They Grinned When the Waiter Spoke to Me in French—but Their Laughter Changed to Amazement at My Reply."[9]

They Laughed When I Sat Down At the Piano But When I Started to Play!—

FIGURE 10.1. John Caples's U.S. School of Music ad.

BEATING UP BULLIES

The ads by Eichler and Caples help to round out the advertising themes of self-improvement and impression management prevalent in the 1920s and 1930s. Two other self-improvement courses were getting their start led by men who would become much more famous than Cody and whose courses are still in existence today: Dale Carnegie and Charles Atlas. The next chapter looks at the life and career of Dale Carnegie. In this section, we focus on bodybuilder Charles Atlas.

It may come as no surprise that the man we know as Charles Atlas was not born with that name. Angelo Siciliano was born in southern Italy in 1892, and his parents brought him to New York in 1905. Growing up in New York, Siciliano settled into a new American name (Charles Siciliano) and a career in leatherwork. He also became an amateur bodybuilder and developed his techniques of isometrics after noticing that lions and tigers at the Bronx Zoo had well-developed muscles but no barbells. Siciliano was also particularly taken with classical body imagery, and he adopted the name Atlas after his friends told him that he resembled a statue of the Greek titan that was on top of the Hotel Atlas in Coney Island. He later even named his children Herc and Diana.

Charles Siciliano's life changed when he entered a photo competition sponsored by Bernarr Macfadden's *Physical Culture* magazine in 1920. In 1921, he also won the Physical Culture contest Macfadden sponsored at New York's Madison Square Garden. Judged by a panel of medical experts, educators, and even an anthropologist, the contest featured a $1,000 prize for the most perfectly developed man, with the winner's measurements preserved for posterity. Charles Atlas went on to a new career as a Coney Island strongman, a pitchman for muscle-developing products, and an artist's model, often for sculptural pieces. According to a *New Yorker* profile, Atlas's torso was the model for busts of George Washington, Alexander Hamilton, and others.[10]

In the 1920s, Charles Atlas and his business partner Charles Roman developed a mail-order bodybuilding course. Toward the end of the nineteenth century, there had been keen interest in physical fitness, promoted by the YMCA and other advocates of what was known as Muscular Christianity.[11] Secular approaches to physical culture emerged, promoted by entrepreneurs like Macfadden, who advocated exercise, fasting and natural foods, fresh air, and sex. In the early 1900s a number of bodybuilders, such as Eugene Sandow, Lionel Strongfort, and Earle E. Liedermann, appealed to boys' and men's insecurities about their physical strength and their bodies. Alois Swoboda even offered "Conscious Evolution" courses with the jarring headline "YOU ARE INFERIOR." Swoboda promised a system that would enable you to "dominate others" and would "double your energy and earning power."[12]

The Charles Atlas course of the 1920s was a relative newcomer to the bodybuilding business, but his advertising had a lighter touch than courses like Swoboda's. Many Atlas ads drew on the self-improvement theme of transformation. They did not focus on book culture or the world of work, but were as much about social success and self-confidence as any other ads of the time. Atlas's ads focused on the efficient transformation from weakling to he-man, alluding to the power of physique in creating a good impression. An ad titled "Life's Most Embarrassing Moment" begins with the sentence "When the girl you were keen about saw you in a bathing suit and yelled 'Hello skinny!'" Another ad led with word and thought balloons: "She said: 'I'm sorry I can't go out with you tonight.' But she really thought 'I'm ashamed to be seen with such a skinny weakling.'" A muscular build—or a muscular boyfriend—was part of the impression one made on others.

The most famous ad was one titled "The Insult that Made a Man out of Mac." In this comic strip ad, an attractive girl and a skinny boy, Mac, are on the beach. The girl is wooed away by a muscular beach bully. After completing the Atlas course, Mac returns to the beach, knocks the bully to the ground, and wins back the girl. The story was variously represented as something that happened to Atlas and something he witnessed at Coney Island, and it presented a before-and-after story in a modern comic-strip format suitable for those who aspired to action rather than reading.[13] Atlas's actual course did involve reading, however, and it came in the form of a dozen lessons written as letters to his students. He provided a regimen of isometric and calisthenic exercises, and he also offered advice on proper food and drink, external and internal cleanliness, fresh air, posture, sleep, and self-control. His exercises and health advice often drew on analogies to nature, religion, and mechanical engineering, and Atlas encouraged his students to think positive thoughts because worry and anger were poisons. He prescribed sunbathing, milk, cold showers, and good music as a mental tonic.[14] Priced at $30 to $35, the course was a great success over the years. Charles Roman served as president of Charles Atlas, Ltd., and handled the business affairs, while Atlas served as the chief spokesman and role model.

That involved public performances such as pulling railroad cars, bending nails and metal rods, and unbending horseshoes. Atlas and Roman understood how to get the public's attention, and one of his feats of strength was a demonstration bending a metal bar at Sing Sing prison in Ossining, New York.

In some ways Cody's course and Atlas's approaches could not have been greater opposites: brain and brawn, book culture and beach culture. Yet they both had the same basic appeal, portraying life as a series of tests in which those with ability, physical or grammatical, were in the best position to seek good fortune and avoid embarrassment. Both claimed to be scientifically tested and were patented (in Cody's case) or trademarked (in Atlas's), and both promised to help users gain autonomy, influence, and admiration. The feats of the inventors were selling points—what Cody did at Gary and what Atlas did at Sing Sing—and each course required just 15 minutes a day. Like Cody's campaign, Atlas's drew on the narratives of self-improvement, the democracy of goods, and first impressions. He offered self-improvement and impression management by means of a better physique, better health, and better prospects for happiness. And his course was quintessentially democratic, requiring no gymnasium and no barbells or special equipment.

When Atlas died in 1972, *The New York Times* reported that his course was still being taken by about 70,000 people annually. Roman, who had become the sole owner in 1969, remained associated with the company for over 70 years until finally selling it in 1997, and the Charles Atlas course is still being offered and advertised today. The phrases Dynamic-Tension and "The Insult That Made a Man out of Mac" are trademarked by Charles Atlas, Ltd., but the Atlas imagery has very much entered the larger sphere of popular culture. The Atlas story is retold in comic-book form in the origin of heroes like Captain America, a weakling rejected as an army recruit but converted to a super-soldier by science and exercise. And the image of a sand-kicking bully was used by

George H. W. Bush to describe Saddam Hussein in 1991. Famous alumni of the course included Mahatma Gandhi's grandson Arun and playwright David Mamet, who has described receiving the lessons in a plain brown wrapper.[16]

From the International Correspondence Schools to the Charles Atlas course, self-improvement products were remarkably successful and popular in the early twentieth century, with a strong appeal to both men and women. We have looked at a few of the many offerings that promised to improve people's lives, but we have only scratched the surface. The advertising of the day promoted books and home-study courses for everything from dancing, shorthand, and cartooning to bust-development to cures for stuttering, smoking, and alcoholism. The *Encyclopædia Britannica* let readers know "There IS an aristocracy in America! It is an Aristocracy of KNOWLEDGE." Nelson Doubleday, Inc., advertised "The Famous Pocket University—A Liberal Reading Education," and Count Rafael Diez de la Cortina offered phonograph records that allowed you to "Speak French at Once!" Not to be outdone, the Rittenhouse Press promoted its 10-volume set on *Woman* with the headline question "How would you like to spend an hour with Cleopatra?"[17]

Correspondence courses and home-study books promised cheap, efficient remedies for modern anxieties. They offered help with career management and with the creation of good impressions. They filled gaps in education and training. As a genre, home-study courses appealed to the American passion for self-improvement, but they also appealed to worry—worry about keeping up in a competitive world of new knowledge, worry about dealing with new social relationships and new values, worry about social correctness, and worry about being judged by others. Advertisers positioned self-improvement products as cures for loneliness, ridicule, weakness, and money troubles, tying together promise and anxiety just as successfully as the old patent medicine ads connected health and illness. Whether you were studying grammar, etiquette, piano, bodybuilding, or the great books, you could become better in the comfort of your home and at your own pace.

Self-Improvement Products

Sherwin Cody's *100% Self-correcting Course, The Book of Etiquette,* the U.S. School of Music, and the Charles Atlas course were just some of the products available to consumers. *The World Almanac and Book of Facts*, like the pulps, for many years contained ad sections. Here is some of what was offered (from *The World Almanac and Book of Facts, 1940*):

Linguaphone is the quick, easy, simple way to speak French, German, Spanish,. . .

High School courses at home (The American School, Chicago, Ill.)

To the man who wants to enjoy an accountant's career (LaSalle Extension University)

I'm having the time of my life—since I learned to dance (Arthur Murray)

A WARNING to men who would like to be independent in the next five years

(Alexander Hamilton Institute)

Just Listen to this Record—Speak Spanish at Once (Cortina Academy)

Government Jobs, pay $1260-$2100 to Start (Patterson School, Rochester, N.Y.)

Learn shorthand in six weeks (School of Speedwriting)

Want a career in photography? (New York Institute of Photography)

Acquire law nights at home (LaSalle Extension University)

US Government Jobs (Franklin Institute, Rochester, N.Y.)

(continued)

You've hoped for it! Now the day has come! (The Harvard Classics)

Large Incomes from Swedish Massage (The College of Swedish Massage)

HE Mailed This Coupon (Charles Atlas)

3 grades of applicants—each one making a definite promotion step (American School)

WORDS can make YOU RICH! (The Grenville Kleiser Course)

Did you ever take an internal bath? (Tyrrell's Hygiene Institute)

ELEVEN

Smile

THE BOOKS AND COURSES OF THE 1920S AND 1930S blended anxieties about the impression one made, the promise of efficiency, and the drive for self-improvement. For a time no single person was more at the center of this than Dale Carnegie, the author of the best-selling *How to Win Friends and Influence People*. Carnegie and Cody shared an advertising agency, Schwab & Beatty, and Victor Schwab managed both of their accounts. Neither Carnegie nor Cody ever mentioned the other in print, and there is no evidence that the two ever met, but if they had run into each other in the waiting room of Schwab & Beatty and compared notes, they would have found that they had much in common.

Dale Carnegie was born in 1888 in rural Missouri, and he grew up on his parents' farm. His parents were poor, devout and hard-working, and Carnegie's mother hoped for him to become a missionary.[1] After graduating from the State Normal School at Warrensburg, where he pursued debate, Carnegie tried his hand at selling courses for the International Correspondence Schools (unsuccessfully) and selling meat products for the Armour company (successfully). To while away the hours when he was on the road in the upper Midwest, he read books on the psychology of salesmanship. In 1910, at the age of 22, Carnegie moved to New York to study acting at the American Academy of the Dramatic Arts and to write. Carnegie failed as an actor and as a novelist—he noted that his manuscript for *The Blizzard* got a reception "as cold as any blizzard that ever howled across the plains of the Dakotas."[2] To support himself in New York, Carnegie began teaching adult education speech courses through the YMCA, where his debate background and acting training helped. As his public speaking course developed and he came to understand what students responded to best, he focused less on formal public speaking and elocution and more on impromptu speaking and on ways to develop enthusiasm and self-confidence.

Like Cody, Carnegie shifted his literary efforts from novels to textbook writing, and in 1910 he coauthored a 512-page textbook with Joseph Berg Esenwein. Their book *The Art of Public Speaking* was a traditional public-speaking text dealing with inflection, voice, precision, gesture, preparation, and memorization, with suggested topics for speakers and an appendix of great political and funeral speeches. There are hints of future ideas, of course. By 1913, Carnegie had a solo book dealing with the techniques of speaking. *Public Speaking and Influencing Men in Business* began with the idea of developing self-confidence and discussed the training and preparation necessary for effective speaking. Carnegie's primary focus was on organization, clarity, and speech techniques, though at the end of each chapter was a section called Speech Building. Here he gave advice on Words Often Mispronounced, Correct Usage, and Errors in English. In *Public Speaking,* Carnegie also included examples of how some historical figures like Benjamin Franklin prepared speeches, and he supplemented those with examples of the speech preparation of contemporary public figures like industrialist Charles Schwab, publisher B. C. Forbes, and President Woodrow Wilson. Carnegie's inspirational profiles of famous people became another means of supporting himself in those days, and in 1934 he published a collection called *Little Known Facts about Well Known People.*[3]

In the mid-1930s, Carnegie was approached by an editor at Simon & Schuster to put together a new book based on his lectures on public speaking. The result blended different perspectives, presenting his ideas with the enthusiastic confidence of the salesman, the authority of a textbook, and the firsthand anecdotes of the celebrity profile. The original *How to Win Friends and Influence People* was made up of five sections, covering human nature and rules for dealing with people, as well as a section on letter writing, which was dropped in later editions. It became a national bestseller by providing advice on overcoming anxiety together with advice on dealing with people—what today we call emotional intelligence. Chapters focused on such topics as "Techniques for Handling People," "Six Ways to Make People Like You," and "Twelve Ways to Win People to Your Way of Thinking." Carnegie advocated giving people a sense of importance by praising them, avoiding arguments, being courteous, and attending to the needs and interests of others. He emphasized such techniques as letting others take ownership of new ideas, supervising by providing indirect criticism, and beginning a sales talk with questions that a person will answer "yes" to. And, he said, you should always smile.

Under Victor Schwab's watchful eye, the ad campaign for Carnegie's course drew on the same model of social anxiety and financial success as Cody's did. The early ads for *How to Win Friends and Influence People,* for example, emphasized the financial value of interpersonal skills. They began this way: "John D. Rockefeller, Sr., once said 'The ability to deal with people is as purchasable a commodity as sugar or coffee. And I will pay more for that ability than for any other under the sun.'" Other ads used the familiar patent medicine approach: they identified the ailment of an inferiority complex and offered a cure. One before-and-after story, for example, told readers about a would-be salesman whose fear of public speaking was cured when he took a Dale Carnegie Course.[4]

Dale Carnegie also had a flair for public relations that Sherwin Cody did not. While Cody became famous through endurance,

Consider the Case of Michael O'Neil

Michael O'Neil lives in New York City. He first got a job as a mechanic, then as a chauffeur.

When he got married, he needed more money. So he tried to sell automobile trucks. But he was a terrible flop. He suffered from an inferiority complex that was eating his heart out.

On his way to see any prospect, he broke out into a cold sweat. Then, before he could get up enough courage to open the door, he often had to walk up and down in front of an office half a dozen times.

When he finally got in, he would invariably find himself antagonizing, arguing. Then he would get kicked out never knowing quite why.

He was such a failure he decided to go back to working in a machine shop. Then one day he received a letter inviting him to attend the opening session of a Dale Carnegie course.

from his many publications and his volume of print advertising, Carnegie took a different, more media-savvy approach. His name was originally spelled Carnagey, but when he rented office space in New York's Carnegie Hall, he adopted the spelling Carnegie. He was also able to cultivate a radio presence because of his friendship with the broadcaster Lowell Thomas, for whom he had once worked. Carnegie also continued to interview the rich and famous for his books and articles, and with the success of *How to Win Friends and Influence People,* he became a celebrity himself.

Carnegie's business model differed from Cody's as well. Cody's school operated from a central headquarters in Rochester, which kept track of students, answered inquiries, mailed course material and books, and billed for tuition. Carnegie adopted a licensing system for his face-to-face course in 1944 that enabled many of his graduates to teach and market his course. He adopted a standardized curriculum of conversational and group techniques together with class sessions in which students gave short presentations from their own experiences. Licensing and standardization also paved the way for the course to continue after Carnegie's death. Dale Carnegie & Associates, Inc., was formed in 1954, and after Carnegie's death in 1955 it was run by Carnegie's widow Dorothy, who headed the company until her death in 1998. While we no longer see print ads for *How to Win Friends and Influence People,* the present-day Dale Carnegie course is thriving.

NOTHING SUCCEEDS LIKE SUCCESS

Carnegie's and Cody's courses differed in another, more fundamental way, in that they emphasized different qualities needed for success. To appreciate the differences fully, we must take a broader look at success rhetoric in America and ways in which the two writers drew on traditional and emerging themes related to self-improvement. Success and self-improvement writing in America has to do with wealth, work, and worth, and its historians have often noted how the themes of religion, character, and personality enter into the genre. Cotton Mather, the influential New England Puritan, first set the tone for colonial success literature with his view that everyone had two callings—a religious calling based on service to God and a personal calling to be useful to one's neighbors. In Mather's view, the two callings should be balanced, and if they were, individuals would be both hardworking and generous. In some ways, Benjamin Franklin was both Mather and anti-Mather. Franklin, born four decades after Mather, promoted a version of success that fit his Pennsylvania Quakerism. In *The Way to Wealth, Advice to a Young Tradesmen,* and his *Autobiography,* Franklin emphasized such qualities of character as hard work and thrift, writing that "The way to wealth, if you desire it, is as plain as the way to market. It depends chiefly on two words; *industry* and *frugality;* that is, waste neither *time* nor *money,* but make the best use of both."[5] Like Mather, Franklin saw work as a means of moral improvement and wealth as a means to an end. But for Franklin, the end goal was not just religious but individualistic as well. Material success permitted the freedom to practice self-improvement by study, conversation, and reading, and the opportunity to improve the condition of others by philanthropy and good works.

Later success and self-improvement rhetoric would often reflect the influence of Franklin's humanitarianism and Mather's religiosity, tending in style more toward Franklin's avuncular approach than Mather's fire and brimstone. Franklin's approach was spread through schoolbooks, conduct manuals, and novels. William H. McGuffey's *Eclectic Readers* taught thrift and work and made the connection between work, wealth, usefulness, and happiness. Henry Ward Beecher's *Lectures to Young Men* promoted the values of work and wealth, and he warned of the many moral pitfalls along the road to success. And Horatio Alger, with his scores of books about boys overcoming adversity, defined a literary genre of young adult success rhetoric that remained popular through World War I. Alger's literary formula involved showing how character qualities of thrift and work would enable young men to compete, grow wealthy, and use their wealth to serve others (Sherwin Cody's *In the Heart of the Hills* was a typical Alger-style tale). Religious interpretations of success and character were also spread through churches. Preachers like Russell H. Conwell, the Baptist minister whose "Acres of Diamonds" speech was popular on the lecture circuit for almost 50 years, claimed that it was a Christian duty to become rich and to put wealth to good use.[6] For Conwell, poverty was a character flaw.

The concentration of wealth in the late nineteenth century also prompted men like Andrew Carnegie and John D. Rockefeller, Sr., to reflect publicly on the stewardship of wealth and its relation to character. Carnegie's famous 1889 essay "Wealth" acknowledged the social friction caused by industrial progress and maintained that the rich had an obligation to give their money away for the good of the poor. Carnegie even argued for a graduated income tax, writing that "Men who continue hoarding great sums all their lives . . . should be made to feel that the community, in the form of the state, cannot thus be deprived of its proper share."[7] John D. Rockefeller, too, subscribed to a version of Carnegie's gospel of wealth, seeing "the power to make money [as] a gift from God to be developed and used to the best of our ability for the good of mankind."[8] Carnegie and Rockefeller began their lives in relative poverty, and as they promoted the Horatio Alger ethic of wealth and stewardship through work, thrift, and piety, they created a powerful cultural image of what success meant.

At the same time, the changing nature of work generated new ideas about the traits of workers and managers. As work shifted from individual agricultural production or craftsmanship to labor in a factory or bureaucracy, managers began to think about workers' character in terms of dedication to assigned tasks. This attitude was exemplified by Elbert Hubbard's famous story "A Message to Garcia," which celebrates a solider who carries out a difficult mission without question or complaint (in that case, getting a message to General Calixto García, the leader of the Cuban insurgents in 1898). Hubbard's story became widely used as a motivational message to employees, promoting and reinforcing the qualities that American business valued at the time. The character of managers and independent businessmen, in turn, was increasingly defined by the notion of service. Since not everyone could become a steward of great wealth like Carnegie or Rockefeller, the next best justification of business was in service. Service encompassed two ideas—adding value commercially by serving customers well, and adding value socially by improving public welfare and doing other good works. The establishment of business service organizations such as the Rotarians, the Lions, and the Kiwanis in the period from 1905 to 1917 reflected this second outlook on success as service to the common good.[9] Cody, for example, subscribed to the service ethic of American business and to the goal of providing "personal service" that had "true value."[10]

This model of success was challenged by novel ideas which suggested alternatives to industriousness, thrift, and service. One came from the New Thought religious movement of the late 1800s, which adapted Christian mysticism, Buddhism, and American transcendentalism. New Thoughters believed that the divine spirit was everywhere as a universal mind and that mind power was the only real power in the world. Tapping mind power, they believed, was the means to success, health, and happiness, and New Thought promoted positive thinking, affirmation, autosuggestion, and visualization in the place of hard work, thrift, and service.

While New Thought was suggesting that all minds were connected, the science of psychology was providing insight from another direction by helping to explain the attitudes and behaviors of other minds. William James had promoted the idea of habit as underlying behavior, and applied psychologists like Harry Overstreet and Walter Dill Scott were suggesting ways that psychology could be applied in advertising and sales to influence people's hopes, desires, and actions. In his 1926 book *Influencing Human Behavior,* for example, Overstreet explained that effective speaking, writing, and persuasion began from the proposition that "What we attend to controls our behavior. What we can get others to attend to controls their behavior," and he offered a variety of practical techniques for getting others to attend to a message.[11] From the applied psychologist's viewpoint, the problem of success was not (or not just) managing and improving oneself, it was dealing with other people. Mind power and psychological understanding soon made their way into the success literature. Historian Warren Susman has described how business advice manuals changed their focus from building character to developing personality. As one example, he points to two books by Orison Swett Marden, the founder of *Success* magazine, which in the course of two decades shifted from mental and moral traits to charm, poise, and likeability.[12] Marden's 1899 volume was *Character: The Greatest Thing in the World;* his 1921 book was titled *Masterful Personality.*

A third factor affecting the literature of success was the shifting nature of work itself. As twentieth-century work became more situated in large organizations and hierarchies, the conditions for success increasingly involved matters of fitting in and understanding others rather than working hard and understanding oneself. By the 1950s, sociologists like C. Wright Mills and William H. Whyte were talking about organizational advancement in terms of one's ability to fit socially, to manage others, and to be managed. Looking specifically at success literature, they found a shift away from individual initiative, hard work, and efficiency. In *The Organization Man,* Whyte wrote that "A half-century ago the usual self-improvement book bore down heavily on the theme of individual effort to surmount obstacles." By the 1950s, however, "what they tell you to do is to adjust to the situation rather than change it." Similarly, in *White Collar,* Mills found that the old entrepreneurial model of success "linked with the sober personal virtues" of perseverance, work, and thrift was giving way to a pattern of success based on "the climb within and between prearranged hierarchies."[13]

Factors like New Thought, applied business psychology, and the white-collar mindset were coming together in new approaches to success in the twentieth century, many of which involved skills of understanding and influencing people, organizations and organizational forces. Where do Carnegie and Cody fit in this evolution? *How to Win Friends and Influence People* was the top-selling nonfiction book in 1937, and it is often seen as a watershed event signaling a new focus on personality and interpersonal communication.[14] Of course, many success, self-improvement, and etiquette works touched on both character and personality, so we should not think of Carnegie's book as marking a sudden shift in success rhetoric from character to personality. Writers like Carnegie and Cody had a toolbox of ideas and images to draw on, and we can look at them not as opposites but rather in terms of their relative focus on certain themes.

Both were grounded in the techniques of business writing, practical teaching, and sales, though with different emphases. The *100% Self-correcting Course* arose from Cody's work as a teacher of letter writing and copywriting rather than public speaking. While he and Carnegie drew on the same ideas about sales psychology, Cody based his psychology in literature as a guide to human reactions, desires, and motivations. Carnegie's sales experience, on the other hand, was face-to-face, and his teaching experience was in terms of classroom work on speech, poise, and presence. His psychological advice was framed in terms of anecdotes from his interviews and personal contacts.

The two approaches reflect a written versus spoken emphasis in other ways. Cody described himself as interested in painting pictures with words, and his perspective on letter writing and advertising was one of mass communication. Carnegie, on the other hand, aimed at solving "the biggest problem you face," which was "dealing with people."[15] Carnegie's book focused on motivating people by building personal relationships, and so his perspective was that of interpersonal communication; he emphasized overcoming the anxiety of speaking, practical negotiation, and motivating and managing others. Cody's perspective in the *100% Self-correcting Course* was largely technical advice aimed at meeting the expectations of correct (linguistic) behavior. This was evident in another way in Cody's success book *Business Practices Up to Date,* which was subtitled *How to Be a Private Secretary* and which explained how to be a good employee.

As a success writer, Cody seemed more firmly rooted in the camp of character than Carnegie was. Cody's 1913 *Principles of Success in Business* discussed efficiency topics such as how to receive and give supervision for maximum effect, but he also included a section on "positive personal qualities" for workers. Here he stressed "clear and careful thinking" as an employee's most important quality but also identified good health (arising from sleep, diet, exercise, cleanliness, and fresh air) and reliability. Cody's focus on reason, health, and reliability falls squarely in the character approach to success. He also included a short section on developing a pleasing personality in his success advice, but his advice on personality is stated in terms of service: "There is only one way to develop a pleasing personality," Cody writes, "and that is to set the mind steadfastly on hope, courage, helpfulness to others who especially need help (helping those who don't need help is sycophancy)." Carnegie's discussion of helpfulness was more instrumental. Carnegie described helpfulness in terms of "wants" rather than "needs," saying that "the only way to influence other people is to talk about what they want and show them how to get it."[16] Describing a university study of business leaders attitudes, Carnegie reported that "85% [of financial success] is due to skill in human engineering—to personality and the ability to lead people." Cody had summarized the same report by saying that "85% of success in any field of business is due *not* to superior business knowledge—but to *superior ability in influencing others.* Since words are the tools we use to accomplish this, how vital it is that you make a masterly command of English YOURS!"[17]

Both Cody and Carnegie were certainly aware of mind power literature. Cody hinted at the power of positive thinking, writing that "everyone must admit that setting the mind resolutely on cheerfulness and success is the greatest possible step toward getting them."[18] There are stronger elements of New Thought in Carnegie's work, including the principle of attracting positive results with positive behavior. And in his later book *How to Stop Worrying and Start Living,* Carnegie described the "magic of thought" and wrote that "the longer I live the more deeply I am convinced of the tremendous power of thought. . . . I know that men and women can banish worry, fear and transform their lives by changing their thoughts. I know! I know!! I know!!!"[19] In *How to Win Friends and Influence People,* however, Carnegie's exposition and principles were psychological, instrumental, and transactional, citing psychologists like William James and Harry Overstreet rather than mind power proponents.[20] His instrumentalism was often mocked by critics (like Sinclair Lewis, who saw the book as teaching people "how to smile and bob and pretend to be interested in people's hobbies so that you might screw them out of things").[21] But Carnegie believed that by showing interest in others, you became interested in them, and he felt that by understanding human relations and getting along with people, you became not just a better manager of people but more confident, sincere, and happy. He had in mind a "New Way of Life" in which people were not merely pretending to be interested in others but changed their personalities to become genuinely interested.[22]

Over the years, Carnegie's emphasis shifted from techniques of public speaking to developing an influential personality to conquering anxiety and worry.[23] Carnegie's trajectory—from skill-building to leadership to happiness—recapitulated in some ways the trajectory of self-improvement literature from self-education to self-help.[24] Cody's approach, on the other hand, was situated in that older tradition of correctness, canon, and work, and his touchstone seems to have been the Harvard Classics. Cody's course and success advice tied the grammatical and literary tradition to business success and personal fulfillment. Sociologist Richard Huber summarized the character and personality approaches by suggesting that "The problem for the character ethic was not people, but the individual's own inner resources," while for the personality ethic "the big obstacles were not in the individual himself . . . , but in the responses of other people."[25] Huber's summary encapsulates the difference between Cody's and Carnegie's emphases as well.

TWELVE

Language, Culture, and Anxiety

CODY'S COURSE WAS A GREAT SUCCESS IN THE 1920S and 1930s, and it continued strong into the 1940s. His ads periodically updated the number of students served, which grew to 50,000 in 1928, 100,000 in 1937, and 150,000 in 1950. Students paid about $30 for the course materials, so we can estimate the gross annual revenue from 1928 to 1937 as averaging $160,000 per year and the revenues from 1938 to 1950 as averaging $125,000 per year.[1] Even accounting for overhead costs associated with the Rochester operation, Cody was making a good income from the *100% Self-correcting Course.*

We have already discussed some of the factors that contributed to the success of the course: the emergence of the advertising industry and the importance of books and magazines. The growth of correspondence education also played a role, and we will look at that in Chapter Fourteen. But the most important condition underlying Cody's success was the long-standing anxiety about correctness in language. As we have seen, Cody's ads appealed directly to insecurity about language and culture and to the social and economic benefit of correct behavior. The background of these linguistic insecurities is our point of departure in this chapter.

The nature of educated speech and correct writing has always been a concern of Americans. In colonial times, writers like Franklin argued that the English of America was not up to the standards of British cultural authorities. Chief among these authorities was Bishop Robert Lowth, one of a group of English writers who attempted to codify grammar in order to slow language change. Lowth's *Short Introduction to English Grammar,* first published in 1762, critiqued usage and promoted the method of teaching by false syntax—that is of teaching by citing examples of errors. Other American writers, such as Thomas Jefferson, resisted English cultural authorities like Lowth. Jefferson instead favored the approach of Joseph Priestly, who proposed to resolve questions of grammar by attention to educated usage and by extension of the regularities already existing in the language. In embracing language change, Jefferson envisioned the American language as a social and moral force that would recognize innovation and that would codify populist rather than privileged usage. He was joined in this preference by Noah Webster, who felt that a uniform American language would promote a national identity. Webster was critical of Lowth and of the English lexicographer Samuel Johnson as well, and he was sympathetic to early nineteenth-century critics who saw them as smothering Anglo-Saxon language traditions with Latinate and French influences.[2]

Throughout the nineteenth century, language issues remained important in the United States. Westward expansion meant that other parts of the country defined themselves in relation to the cultural centers of the East. In this expansion, language was a means of social status, and books codified and promoted linguistic information. Authoritative language increasingly came to be that which was approved by dictionary-makers and grammarians. And while books on grammar and usage had an American flavor and used American spellings, they were still often largely based on the tradition established by Lowth. Lowth's works themselves were not intended for widespread school use, but both his rules and methods were soon adapted by popularizers such as Lindley Murray, one of the best-selling authors of his time, whose grammar books sold over sixteen million copies.

Grammars and dictionaries had a continually strong market, but the advance of book learning in the United States in the nineteenth century was double-edged. As historian Kenneth Cmiel has emphasized, schooling and the sale of home dictionaries and grammars spread the authority of linguistic refinement but undermined that authority at the same time. As more people became familiar with the prescriptions of traditional grammar, the variance of their everyday speech from those prescriptions became apparent. People naturally wondered what was so wrong with the way they talked, and the emphasis on politely literary English was increasingly associated with pretentiousness and elitism.[3] The tendency toward anti-elitism can be illustrated by reaction to the language style of Andrew Jackson, who was perhaps the first American president to embody the colloquial style. By the time he was president, Jackson could shift his style from informal to refined depending on his audience. But as linguist Allan Metcalf notes, Jackson was portrayed by his political opponents as a poor speaker and writer. John Quincy Adams, Jackson's rival for the presidency in 1824 and 1828, referred to him as "a barbarian who cannot write a sentence of grammar and can hardly spell his own name." The focus on Adams's greater formal education, however, largely backfired. Metcalf reports the story of a farmer who was persuaded by an Adams supporter that Adams was the better-educated candidate. The farmer nevertheless declared he would vote for Jackson, saying "I never found a dictionary man that wasn't half a fool. I'm for Hickory, I believe."[4] True or apocryphal, the anecdote illustrates the way in which refinement was portrayed as foolish affectation rather than cultural authority, and in the election of 1828, Adams carried the New England states and Jackson most of the rest of the country.

In the United States, language was linked to the question of who had the right to be heard and taken seriously. Fault lines existed between East and West, North and South, rural and cosmopolitan, educated and unschooled, male and female, black and white, and immigrant and native. Attention to language differences was intensified by the spread of popular culture in the nineteenth century. The growth of newspapers and the penny press, for example, favored the tastes of a broad readership rather than a narrow one, and it established a natural medium for colloquial speech and diverse voices. Populist editor Horace Greeley aimed his *New York Tribune* at a mass audience and was an early and vigorous defender of the colloquial. His paper and his own editorials were noted both for slang and for common, direct language. The competing *New York Times* criticized Greeley's paper by writing that "We see no reason why the language of a newspaper should be different from the language of decent society, from the language used by gentlemen in their daily intercourse."[5] American fiction was coming into its own as well, and writers like Charles F. Browne, George Washington Harris, and of course Mark Twain used slang and dialect stylistically. In his essay "Concerning the American Language," Twain wrote that standards of language could no longer come from "that little corner called New England" and that a nation's language "is not simply a manner of speech obtaining among the educated handful, the manner obtaining among the vast uneducated multitude must be considered also."[6]

The debate about usage was also evident in the marketing of dictionaries, which were increasingly popular among the growing professional class and in schools. The country's best-known lexicographer, Noah Webster, was perceived by many as a linguistic radical for his idiosyncrasies of spelling and etymology. By mid-century, Webster's dictionary saw stiff competition from *The Universal and Critical Dictionary of the English Language* published in 1846 by Joseph Worcester, a one-time employee and long-time rival.[7] Eventually the Webster camp prevailed, largely by winning school contracts in the East and later in the Midwest. As new editions of Webster's and Worcester's dictionaries appeared, their differences grew smaller. But for several years, as the rival camps battled for market share, partisan reviews appeared in the national press. The reviews are interesting not so much in determining which dictionary was better, but in what the public expected. A dictionary was seen as a conservative text, preserving the form of language in order to ensure civil behavior. As *The New York Times* wrote in 1860:

> There are thousands of words used colloquially, or in newspapers, or belonging to the repository of slang, whose incorporations in work claiming to be *arbiter elegantiarum* of speech would be either needless or positively objectionable.[8]

The spread westward also created new cultural images of coarse cowboy language, and frontier teachers and ministers took up the challenge of bringing Eastern values westward. William Chauncey Fowler, a Webster son-in-law, warned in his 1868 *English Grammar* that "As our countrymen are spreading westward across the continent, and are brought into contact with other races, and adopt new modes of thought, there is some danger that, in the use of their liberty, they may break loose from the laws of the English language, and become marked not only by one, but by a thousand Shibboleths."[9] Back in the East, cities were perceived as problem areas, and urban dialect was criticized by writers like Jacob Riis as a multiethnic garble and a source of the careless speech of the native working class.[10] The speech of rural youths, many of whom had migrated to cities and developed new usage habits, also raised concerns, as did the speech of foreigners, workers, businessmen, and the middle class, all of which supposedly showed signs of declining intellectual and moral standards. Writers and scholars took up the cause of defending refined speech in newspaper articles, lectures, and books. For example, George Perkins Marsh's *Lectures on the English Language,* published in 1860, argued that popular literature had grievously injured the language and morals of the country and that "To pillory such offenses, to point out their absurdity, to detect and expose the moral obliquity which too often lurks beneath them, is the sacred duty of every scholar."[11] In a similar vein, language purist Edward Gould collected his newspaper and magazine essays as the book *Good English* in 1867, especially targeting misused words. Richard Grant White's popular 1870 book *Words and Their Uses* also focused on supposedly misused words such as *donate* and *jeopardize.*[12] And William Matthews published *Words, Their Use and Abuse* in 1876, condemning "all inaccuracies of speech" and adding the patriotic warning that "the corrupter of a language stabs straight at the very heart of his country."[13] While Marsh, Gould, White, and Matthews defended refined speech against supposed grammatical and moral corruption, others were developing practical tools for guiding and correcting writers and journalists. In 1877 William Cullen Bryant published his *Index Expurgatorius,* a list of incorrect and vulgar words not to be used in his paper. And Thomas Embly Osmun, using the pseudonym Alfred Ayres, published *The Verbalist* in 1881, the first alphabetical dictionary of usage.

These writers were a learned group. Marsh was a diplomat, Whig congressman, and early environmentalist. Gould was a writer and translator. White was a Shakespeare scholar, journalist, and musician, and Matthews had been a professor of rhetoric at the University of Chicago. Bryant was a poet and editor-in-chief of the *New York Evening Post,* and Osmun was writer on orthoepy, elocution, and manners as well as grammar. They wrote for the general readers whose language, the authors believed, most needed monitoring and correction, and the period from 1880 to 1900 saw over 100 manuals of usage published in the United States. As Kenneth Cmiel notes, "Verbal critics identified particular errors with policemen, maids, waiters, clerks, shopkeepers in the Bowery, entrepreneurs in general, rural schoolteachers (male), farmers, wives of farmers, popular editors, labor leaders, politicians, the young of virtually every social class, and the nouveau riche both male and female."[14]

Grammar and usage were moving from the schoolhouse to the general public and the workplace, guided by a literary elite. However as the nation and the prosperity of the middle class grew, correct speech could no longer be seen as that of a homogeneous refined class. The best communicators would be those, like Jackson and Lincoln, who were comfortable with both the refined and the colloquial and who could shift among styles appropriate to audience and purpose. As society became more complex and heterogeneous, communication and commerce would involve interactions across lines of class, geography, race, and gender. By the twentieth century, the colloquial was emerging as the norm for the popular press, magazines, business communication, and advertising. These verbal critics, however, would both lose and win their battle. Even as practical language was gaining new authority in publishing, advertising, and political speech, the verbal criticism of nineteenth-century writers like Marsh and White would remain a touchstone, contrasting a culture of refinement with a mass culture. In 1905, for example, Henry James condemned American speech, blaming common schools and newspapers which were "excellent for diffusion, for vulgarization, [and] for simplification"...and "quite below the mark for discrimination and selection, for those finer offices of vigilance and criticism."[15] In dictionaries, usage books, and newspapers, there was an ongoing tension between refinement and populism. Elegant language was portrayed by its advocates as having the potential to transform the common person into someone of learning. Colloquial language, on the other hand, was viewed by its advocates as establishing bonds of communication among real people in a world with practical concerns.

This tension between refinement and populism is a classic problem of usage, and it was one that Sherwin Cody had to contend with as he began to teach English usage. Cody recognized that language was important to anyone wishing to be distinguished from the unrefined masses, and he emphasized this when he noted to potential students that they would "gain a mark of breeding which will persist in you as long as you live."[16] At the same time, Cody's work in advertising and business writing led him to favor the colloquial style and to pronounce that "traditional rules of rhetoric are dead, useless baggage when it comes to getting practical results."[17]

The divide between the refined and popular was not unique to language, of course. As we have seen, it existed in literature, and the same distinction between popular and refined can be found in the fine and performing arts. As historian Lawrence Levine has emphasized, for much of the nineteenth century the arts in America blended popular and refined themes. Levine notes that, with little to choose from, elite and common audiences attended the same cultural events, and audiences often responded to plays and concerts in much the same way that mass audiences respond to sporting events today—by cheering, booing, singing along, and occasionally throwing things at performers. In time, however, the appreciation of refined culture became professionalized by elite interpreters in the same way that language had been a century earlier. Levine writes that "Just as Shakespeare was increasingly portrayed as a complex writer whom readers could comprehend only if they armed themselves with a plethora of study aids, so too was the sophistication and difficulty of all aspects of culture driven home continually."[18] He sees the division of the arts into high and low as part of a larger "sacralization of culture" which allowed their signifying and transformative aspects to be emphasized.[19] High and low culture provided a way of identifying people by their choices of entertainment and their behavior in theatres, concert halls, museums, and libraries. But there was also the potential for social transformation: exposure to book culture, the arts, and refined language could increase the sensitivity and the interests of the common people.

For many, Cody was a guide in this social transformation. In an age in which people felt increasingly pressed to be educated

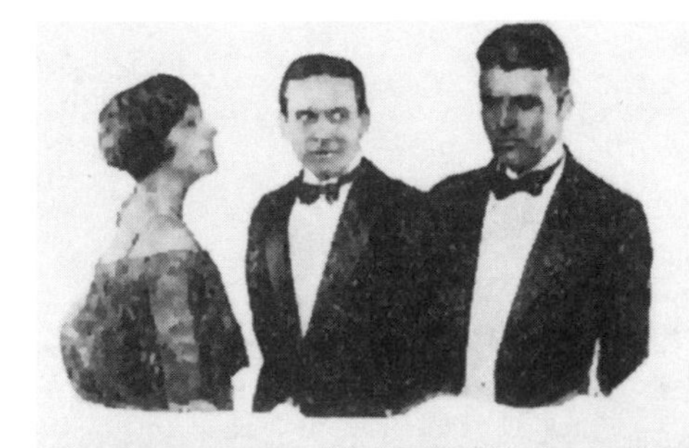

FIGURE 12.1. A Cody ad stressing anxiety.

and aware of both correct language and the world of books, Cody offered himself as a modern, practical guide. He did not seek to convert readers into highbrows, but he could help them to avoid being seen as lowbrows with his businesslike approach to language and literature. He offered a transformative introduction for the uneducated and an efficient refresher for the more cosmopolitan.

THIRTEEN

Linguistics and the New Rhetoric

SHERWIN CODY WAS NOT THE ONLY ONE THINKING about the English language in new ways, of course. Language had been professionalized much earlier than art and culture, by Lowth, Murray, and others, and by the late nineteenth century scholars were rethinking the prescriptive tradition. The frontiers of knowledge were expanding in nearly all fields. New developments were coming forward in the sciences due to the work of Darwin, Wallace, Mendel, and others, and in psychology and philosophy due to the work of people like William James, Charles Peirce, and Sigmund Freud. And American and European linguistics was establishing a new foundation as well. In 1786, Sir William Jones, a British jurist living in India, had sparked interest in the comparative histories of languages with the publication of his book *The Sanscrit Language*. Scholars began to understand language change as Jakob Grimm, Karl Verner, and others formulated correspondences among related languages, and work on comparative linguistics uncovered the vast Indo-European family tree which linked many of the languages of Europe and the East.

Linguists started to think about change as a feature of contemporary languages as well. By the late 1800s, thinkers like

Ferdinand de Saussure and Max Müller in Europe and William Dwight Whitney in the United States were beginning to treat language as a system of social signs, and they were establishing the groundwork for a science of language that would stand as its own discipline. The linguistics of Saussure, Müller, and Whitney diverged from both literature and rhetoric, and the three fields came to have quite different approaches to language. While some literary scholars, such as Whitney's student Thomas Lounsbury, did sophisticated work in both linguistics and literature, many others labored under the oversimplifications of usage critics who saw the language as steadily decaying. Such critics, as noted in the preceding chapter, were committed to using and preserving the most refined literary language, and they tended to see correct language, logical thought, serious literature, and proper morality as going together. The new discipline of linguistics had a more complicated and democratic understanding of language variation. The lexicographic, folklore, and dialect study traditions that influenced linguistics recognized creative influences outside of refined literature. These traditions led linguists to see different types of language as being legitimately suited to different functions. In America, Whitney pioneered a view of correctness as a matter of fashion rather than authoritative tradition. His 1867 *Language and the Study of Language* and later works explained the primacy of speech over writing, the naturalness of language change, the relativism of usage, and the descriptive role of the grammarian.[1] Early twentieth-century educators like George Philip Krapp, Sterling A. Leonard, and Fred Newton Scott developed these views further and brought the idea of a new science of language to teacher training in the English language arts.

Promoting linguistics among teachers was a slow and difficult task, however. Many schools taught grammar using the methods of Lowth and Murray, and teachers were influenced by the still popular Richard Grant White and William Matthews, whose ideas were reiterated by such cultural authorities as Henry James. At the beginning of the twentieth century, schools stressed traditional grammar and elocution. In fact, when an Alabama teacher established *Better Speech Week* in 1916, proper pronunciation became a national phenomenon in schools. *Better Speech Week* even included a pledge linking pronunciation and patriotism and echoing concerns about un-American influences:

> I love the United States of America. I love my country's flag. I love my country's language. I promise: That I will not dishonor my country's speech by leaving off the last syllable of words. That I will say a good American "yes" and "no" in place of an Indian grunt "um-hum" and "nup-um" or a foreign "ya" or "yeh" and "nope." That I will do my best to improve American speech by avoiding loud rough tones, by enunciating distinctly, and by speaking pleasantly, clearly and sincerely.[2]

Much of the early twentieth-century debate on linguistics in English education took place in the National Council of Teachers of English (known by the acronym NCTE). Its *English Journal* debuted in 1912 with an emphasis on grammatical terminology and on proper—British—pronunciation. Most writers for the *Journal,* and doubtless many readers as well, thought that a uniform style of correct grammar and pronunciation was best taught through drills and the memorization of rules. A minority, however, favored tolerance of dialect and variation, seeing American speech as both natural and vigorous, and this minority pointed out that textbook grammar rules were very often at odds with actual educated usage. In 1917 Fred Newton Scott provided a defense of American speech as opposed to British. In 1918 George Philip Krapp discussed unrealistic aspirations for speech, and Sterling Leonard critiqued "Old Purist Junk."[3] Scott, Krapp, and Leonard advocated research on actual usage as the means of developing standards of speech and writing, rather than reliance on drills of eighteenth century prescriptions. But linguistics was slow to take hold. When Ella Heaton Pope argued in a 1919 article for linguistics to be a required subject in college and high school, much of her *English Journal* article had to be devoted to simply defining what linguistics was.[4]

The traditionalist viewpoint and the new scientific one aroused considerable debate among English educators. At first prescriptivism was widely favored, and from 1920 to 1923 articles in favor of traditional approaches led by about four to one.[5] However, the progressives were undeterred, and the 1920s saw a number of statistical studies of actual usage, by Leonard, Charles Fries, and others, as well as the completion in England of the *New English Dictionary* (now called the *Oxford English Dictionary*), a work based on historical principles rather than prescriptive ones. By 1929, the NCTE Committee on Language Courses had gotten to the point of recommending training in phonetics, the history of English, and modern linguistics.

Although proponents of traditionalism have sometimes portrayed linguists as advocating that one usage is as good as another, this wasn't the case at all. Krapp, for example, argued that good English "has to do with the effective applications of language, especially with the bond of union between the speaker or writer and the rest of the world."[6] And Leonard advocated that grammar instruction should follow the usage of educated speakers rather than of dated authorities, and thus should change as educated speakers changed their habits. In order to be authoritative about good English, Krapp and Leonard argued, it was necessary to understand actual usage. Sherwin Cody was a frequent contributor to the *English Journal* in its first decade, and though he did not participate in linguistic debates, he was sympathetic to the approach of linguists. In his 1912 *English Journal* article on "Scientific Principles in the Teaching of Composition," Cody had approvingly cited Thomas Lounsbury's article "Compulsory Composition in Colleges," which had explained that "grammar is nothing but the generalization of the facts of utterance, so rhetoric is nothing but the generalization of the facts of style."[7] Cody also cited Krapp, Leonard, and British phonetician Daniel Jones later in *The New Art of Writing and Speaking the English Language.* There Cody wrote that while he had already recognized the importance of the colloquial standard in the 1903 edition of *The Art of Writing and Speaking the English Language,* Leonard had shown the colloquial to be endorsed by the "highest authorities," including Otto Jespersen, C. T. Onions, and Krapp, as well as by authors like Booth Tarkington and H. G. Wells and editors like H. L. Mencken and William Allen White.[8]

Cody was no theoretician, of course, but his sentiments on language and grammar ran parallel to those of the modern linguists. He understood the standard language to be both a social construct and a social necessity. In *Commercial Tests and How to Use Them,* for example, he wrote that businesses expect employees to follow fashion in language as well as clothing. One's English should be "correct without attracting attention, and so win the approval of educated people without raising the suspicions of the uneducated."[9] In *The New Art,* Cody commented further on how this viewpoint was a break from the past:

> The standard of correct English usage has changed slowly but steadily since the opening of the twentieth century. In times past, the educational world has felt a necessity for teaching and trying to maintain the formal literary standard, according to which many common colloquial expressions are condemned... [In modern times, however, it] is infinitely more important... to know what good colloquial usage is than what so-called formal literary usage ought to be. The ordinary person is no longer misled into supposing that his everyday speech should conform to the rules of literary standards.[10]

Like progressive linguists, Cody recognized the value of actual usage and criticized the practices of the schools. His "Scientific Principles in the Teaching of Composition" argued that "with a false hypercriticism, we are actually teaching innumerable errors—we are condemning as improprieties the fundamental idioms of the language."[11] Cody held to this position throughout his life, reiterating it in his advertisements and (32 years later) in his *Coaching Children in English*. The National Council of Teachers of English came to a similar conclusion, and by 1936 its Curriculum Committee recommended that the teaching of grammar apart from writing be discontinued.[12] By the 1960s, many classroom educators had come to this conclusion as well.[13] The criticism that teaching grammar as a separate subject does not improve writing was sometimes misunderstood as the attempt to do away with grammar, but this was not Cody's intent or that of the linguists. Rather, the common goal of Cody and of Krapp, Scott, Leonard, and others was to improve the teaching of grammar, not to eliminate it.

Though Cody embraced the colloquial standard, his publications were outside of the academic discourse written for teachers, opinion leaders, and scholars. Cody wrote primarily for businessmen, for home-study English students, and later for parents, and to the extent that he was noticed by linguists, he seems to have been dismissed on a misreading of his approach as rigidly prescriptive. In his 1918 condemnation of language purists, Sterling Leonard offered a blanket condemnation of manuals of business English, saying that "misconceived dicta about usage are to be found in newspaper style sheets and in manuals of business English—places above all others where one would naturally look for guides to practically effective expression."[14] Many years later, Robert A. Hall, Jr., in his book *Linguistics and Your Language,* took Cody to task more explicitly. Hall began the chapter called "Right vs. Wrong" with a mock Cody ad. He remarked that "those who talk or advertise in this way and offer to cure our errors in pronunciation or grammar are simply appealing to our sense of insecurity with regard to our own speech."[15] Hall viewed purism as socially divisive, saw prescriptive rules as misguided, and advocated standardizing changes that had become widespread. At the same time, however, he acknowledged the social reality of norms:

> Often enough, we may find we need to change our usage, simply because social and financial success depends on some norm, and our speech is one of the things that will be used as a norm. In a situation like this, it is advisable to make the adjustment; but let's do so on the basis of the actual social acceptability of our speech, not because of the fanciful prescriptions of some normative grammarian or other pseudo-authority.[16]

Hall's linguistic realism accepted norms as fashion rather than higher logic or morality. The irony of Hall's criticism is that he and Cody both disdained pedantic authority and shared a view of language as a social and economic tool. In *Commercial Tests and How to Use Them,* for example, Cody emphasized the utility of language and its social differentiation, making the same point as Hall in a more colorful fashion:

> The person who is a good talker and a correct writer will often pass for a college graduate, though only a high school graduate. On the other hand, what contempt people have for college graduates (of whom there are all too many) who can't write a decent letter, or who talk like baseball players, or beauty shop sales girls.[17]

FROM RHETORIC TO COMPOSITION

At the same time that modern linguistics was emerging, changes were coming about in the related discipline of rhetoric as well. In the early nineteenth century, rhetoric instruction was largely defined by the model of Hugh Blair's *Lectures on Rhetoric and Belles-Lettres*. First published in 1783, Blair's *Lectures* were just that—a compilation of 47 lectures given to students at the University of Edinburgh, ranging over such topics as "Taste," "The Sublime in Writing," "Means of Improving Eloquence," and "Epic Poetry."[18]

Blair's approach blended writing and oratory together as governed by taste, which he saw as arising from a natural capacity to respond to beauty that could be trained by the study and appreciation of literature. For Blair, moral and aesthetic processes had a common foundation in proportion and balance, and morals and aesthetics developed in tandem.[19] But Blair also stressed conventions of taste as a way to take part in educated discussion and to avoid social stigma. In Lecture 1, for example, he wrote:

> In an age when works of genius and literature are so frequently the subjects of discourse, when every one erects himself into a judge, and when we can hardly mingle in polite society without bearing some share in such discussions; studies of this kind, it is not to be doubted, will appear to derive part of their importance from the use to which they may be applied in furnishing materials for those fashionable topics of discourse, and thereby enabling us to support a proper rank in social life.[20]

Blair's lectures were successful not just for their advice on spoken eloquence and written style but because they linked taste with success. In the United States, editions of Blair's book became especially popular classroom texts, and many included recitation questions appended after the lectures. Books like Blair's were very much aimed at those who already had a high degree of literacy and an understanding of grammar. However, it gradually became clear that rhetoric separate from practical composition instruction did little to improve writing, and after the Civil War higher education began to link rhetoric, grammar, and composition in new ways.[21] Harvard University in particular was a catalyst for change under the presidency of our old friend Charles W. Eliot. As president, Eliot was quick to point out the weakness of English studies, arguing in his 1869 inaugural address that "English should be studied from the beginning of school life to the end of college life," and he maneuvered to place it on a par with instruction in the classical languages.[22] Harvard imposed an English composition entrance requirement on the entering class of 1874, requiring a literary essay that demonstrated correctness in spelling, punctuation, grammar, and expression. By 1882, Harvard had added a requirement that applicants be able to correct "specimens of bad English" given in the entrance examination.[23] The intent of the entrance examinations was to refocus preparatory schools and high schools on correctness in writing, so that the university could continue to devote itself to higher learning. The prep schools and high schools accommodated by adding more essay writing to their curricula, but many students—as many as half—still fell short in the exams. In 1885 Harvard instituted a temporary course that combined the reading of model essays with practice in theme writing. The course was intended to be in existence only until new students could meet the admissions standards, so it was not given any more descriptive name than English A. Other universities followed Harvard's lead, both in the exams and in adding coursework, and by 1890 a freshman composition requirement existed at most universities. However, remediation and the daily theme approach were unpopular with Harvard faculty and, as the idea spread, with English professors elsewhere.

One result was the development of a new university workforce of graduate students and writing instructors to teach the freshman courses that many professors of literature were—or claimed to be—unable to teach. Another result involved the nature of the course. Since the early freshman composition classes sometimes had over 100 students, the pressure to grade on superficialities was considerable. The task of grading many sets of short essays led to the quickest means of grading possible: correcting errors in grammar, usage, punctuation, and spelling.[24] The emphasis on correctness also affected how writing and grammar were taught: teaching focused on forms and rules. There were of course rules for the avoidance of error in expression—for the mechanics of writing. There were rules for the organization and development of the final product, the formulaic five-paragraph essay. As composition became broadly institutionalized, the kinds of essays assigned also shifted from the abstract to the personal and to simple modes of expression, such as narration, exposition, argument, and persuasion, rather than literary, historical, or philosophic essays. The positive result of the new rhetoric was that the teaching of writing involved more actual production of student essays. The negative result was that it did so by emphasizing superficialities.

Cody understood the limits of teaching writing by correcting errors, and he understood that marking essays was both time-intensive for teachers and of limited effectiveness for students. Other than his comments on his Amherst education and John Genung's traditional rhetoric text, Cody did not write about the college curriculum, but in the *English Journal,* he set forth a proposal for composition study in the high schools. There he argued that the conventional rhetorical modes of exposition, narrative, description, and argumentation were "so artificial as to be useless."[25] In their place, he advocated that the first year of high school English begin with exercises modeling business correspondence. This, he thought, would allow students to practice an easy form of exposition stylistically connected to conversational English. The second year's work would involve "the rewriting of selections from the standard authors," and the third year would focus on condensing and adapting short fiction (for example, "changing one of Maupassant's stories from a Paris setting to an American setting and character").[26] The senior year would shift back from literature to business writing. Cody saw career preparation as the legitimate basis of the curriculum, and his proposal blended the vocational with the literary. Seeing the two as having common goals, he argued:

> No better modern practical application of argumentation can be found than in the study of salesmanship and advertisement writing. America is a business nation. Our education is urged largely as a good preparation for success in doing business. . . . It would be

> difficult to choose better work for the last year in the high school than practical sales letter writing, oral salesmanship talks, and the writing of careful advertisements . . .[27]

As he developed his views on rhetoric and education, Cody naturally drew on and reacted to the work of his teacher John Franklin Genung, who had emerged as a significant theorist of rhetoric. Genung's *Practical Elements of Rhetoric* was first published in 1885, and it was the work that Cody studied carefully and reproduced with his hectograph to sell to his classmates. Genung modernized the approach of Blair, dividing *Practical Elements* into sections on style and invention. Invention, in Genung's view, had to do with the selection of the appropriate mode of writing for a particular purpose—description for the portrayal of objects, narration for the recounting of events, exposition and argumentation for establishing and substantiating the truth. Genung also emphasized the role of practical psychology in invention, seeing rhetoric as "the art of adapting discourse, in harmony with its subject and occasion, to the requirements of the reader or hearer" and distinguishing types of writing as appealing to the intellect, emotions, and will.[28] Genung preferred to write about invention rather than grammar, but in his *Outlines of Rhetoric* he gave 125 rules for correct grammar and included a glossary of frequently misused phrases.[29] The book was mildly reformist as grammars go, stressing brevity in the formulation of rules, the presentation of rules as clusters of related ideas, and their statement as things to do rather than things not to do. Genung also pioneered the technique of numbering the rules in an appendix, which provided "the main procedures of the rhetorical art in a nutshell" and which made marking papers more efficient, since teachers could note the number of the rule in the margin rather than writing corrections.[30]

Genung's influence can be found in several of the ideas that Cody took up in his course. The distinction between critical rhetoric and constructive rhetoric that appears in Cody's *The Art of Writing and Speaking,* for example, is from Genung's works. Genung saw criticism as disciplining a writer's taste and perceptions, while the constructive rhetoric of invention and adaptation actually developed the ability to write. Cody of course took Genung's ideas of constructive rhetoric in a different direction, setting aside the traditional modes and emphasizing news writing, advertising, and business correspondence. Genung had also stressed rhetoric as a liberal art and "concerned, as real authorship must be, not with a mere grammatical analysis... but with the whole man."[31] This too is reflected in Cody's advocacy of literature and rhetoric as the foundation of psychology, conversation, human relations, and a satisfying life.

Genung may have had another influence as well. For a time in the early 1900s, the Amherst professor was associated with the Home Correspondence School of Springfield, Massachusetts. The school offered courses in an Academic and Preparatory Department, an Agricultural Department, a Commercial Department, and a Normal and Common School Department. According to an article in the *New York Observer and Chronicle,* the faculty was made up of about two dozen scholars from "Harvard, Yale, Cornell and other leading institutions."[32] Genung's photo was featured in ads in the *System* and other magazines, and he headed the English curriculum which prepared students for college. Genung's involvement in correspondence education may have spurred Cody's own efforts in this direction as well. But while Cody held Genung in high regard and was certainly influenced by his former teacher's views, Cody saw limitations in Genung's approach. Cody did not see the comprehensiveness of Genung's *Practical Elements* or *Outlines* as suited to modern students' needs. Instead, Cody reduced the grammar in his course to a few points and emphasized the interactive gamelike method of self-test exercises. Cody organized his approach so that students knew where they stood and could measure their

FIGURE 13.1. A Cody ad stressing method.

progress toward the practical goal of eliminating their personal errors. Such a method, in his view, made the teaching of grammar and language more transparent and also more interesting to students by taking their knowledge into account. Cody even advertised it as fun.

FOURTEEN

Study at Home

THE INTELLECTUAL ENVIRONMENT IN WHICH Sherwin Cody worked distinguished practical introductory work from theoretical specialties, and Cody's work was clearly the former. Another crucial educational trend supporting his course was the spread of correspondence learning. As mentioned earlier, correspondence education had taken root in the United States in the late 1800s. Organizations like the Society to Encourage Studies at Home promoted home-study groups, complete with rules and reading guides much like today's middle-class book groups. Cornell University, in rural Ithaca, New York, founded a short-lived Correspondence University in 1883 to serve graduates, teachers, the military, and those preparing for civic service exams, among others. A few years earlier, in 1879, Yale professor William Rainey Harper had organized a summer language institute as part of the Chautauqua Camp Meeting Association in New York, and he began to develop a correspondence course to allow students to continue language study after the summer session was over.

When Harper became president of the newly established University of Chicago in 1892, correspondence education became a feature of that university's extension division. Education by mail took hold in other midwestern universities as well, where many potential students were place-bound and rural. The University of Wisconsin became a leader in correspondence instruction, and one of its most popular correspondence courses was taught by historian Frederick Jackson Turner, who viewed correspondence education as "carrying irrigating streams of education in to the arid regions."[1] Programs also sprang up at the Universities of Nebraska, Kansas, Minnesota, Texas, Missouri, Colorado, Oregon, California, Pennsylvania, and Indiana. Even New York's Columbia University offered home-study college and college-preparatory work, recruiting students with full-page ads in *The New York Times* offering "the advantages of University Instruction" adjusted to the needs of individual students.[2] The student body for correspondence education included immigrants, African-Americans, women, veterans, rural teachers, and prisoners. During the Depression, correspondence education expanded further as classes were offered to Works Progress Administration clients and in Civilian Conversation Corps camps. When the University of Wisconsin offered its correspondence courses to military personnel in 1941, the U.S. Armed Forces Institute began. By 1946, Foxhole University, as it came to be known, offered about 400 credit and noncredit courses.[3]

There were, of course, academic critics of correspondence education. Sociologist Thorstein Veblen, for example, viewed the University of Chicago's efforts in correspondence education as being outside the mission of higher education.[4] And Abraham Flexner, in his 1930 book *Universities: American, English, German,* criticized the quality of correspondence courses at Columbia and Chicago as well as the ethics of their marketing. Flexner wrote that "it is absurd to suppose that to the hordes of extension and home study students registered at Columbia any such opportunity can be offered without lowering of standards."[5] In part because of the ambivalence within traditional universities, correspondence education grew as private business in the first half of the twentieth century rather than a university enterprise.

In a sense, private correspondence education began underground—from the needs of mine workers. In 1891, Thomas J. Foster, the owner of the *Mining Herald,* began offering correspondence courses to help miners pass new state examinations. His offerings soon expanded to hundreds of areas. At the turn of the century, an internal assessment report on International Correspondence Schools' graduates listed over thirty separate ICS "schools" ranging from Chemistry and Civil Service to Electrotherapeutics and Mercantile Decoration. The report noted that students were "as a rule, young men between the ages of 23 and 27 years," and it even listed the names and address of 54,500 students who had done satisfactory work in a third of their courses. The total number of cumulative enrollees in 1905 was 650,000, and ICS saw its 12.7% success rate as good (even "astounding" and "extraordinary"), given the extenuating factors such as student preparation, motivation, time, study habits, and incentives. The report also suggested that the results should be viewed in light of the fact that "many of our students are foreigners, with only a slightest acquaintance with the English language."[6]

Private correspondence education was seen by its advocates as responding to the new social and economic needs of the country in a way that traditional colleges did not. In a speech presented at the 20th-anniversary ICS banquet in 1911, the keynoter, Reverend Joseph H. Odell, discussed "The International Correspondence Schools as a National Asset." Odell described the American economic situation as involving "intelligent discontent" among the working classes, a rising cost of living, social ambition, immigration, and both industrial and efficiency revolutions. Traditional colleges were of limited help in training workers, since colleges "had been grinding out graduates with practically the same culture that they gave centuries before—a broad, ennobling and enriching culture of the mind in language and literature."[7] And even as some colleges retooled toward technology and engineering, Odell noted that they were not at all positioned to help those workers who could not devote four years of time to on-campus college studies. In his view, correspondence education, and ICS specifically, would provide America's new skilled workforce. Cowpunchers, mule drivers, mill workers, and deckhands would be retrained as architects, engineers, and managers, and ICS would be "the saviour of industrial America."[8]

ICS tracked the success of students. Then as now, part of the marketing of long-distance education involved establishing credibility. Cody understood this need as well, since his early work with the National Business Standards Association had been aimed at providing both standards and credibility for business education. He kept track of student completions and asked satisfied students to volunteer feedback and testimonials. As private correspondence education expanded, not all schools maintained the same standards, however. John Noffsinger estimated that by 1926, there were about 350 private correspondence schools in the United States, with total annual revenues of 70 million dollars, and he calculated that four times as many students were enrolled in correspondence schools as were enrolled in traditional colleges and universities.[9] In his view, "an appallingly large proportion of the schools" were "little better than frauds."[10] Noffsinger pointed out that some private correspondence schools were diploma mills offering dubious PhD degrees, that others were teaching bogus healing arts such as "electro-theraputics" and "masso-therapy," and that some were offering instruction in vocational areas not at all suited to correspondence learning. Noffsinger also criticized the business practices of some schools, calling the overemphasis on sales "the most serious criticism to be made against the system of correspondence education." He suggested stronger licensing of correspondence schools, and his National Home Study Council, founded in 1926, helped to set standards for correspondence education and to provide consumer advice.[11] By the 1920s and 1930s, many states had begun to regulate correspondence course sales with fraud laws.

Education researchers would also look critically at correspondence school curricula. In 1938, Ella Woodyard studied

13 correspondence schools as part of a research project for the American Association for Adult Education. Woodyard (or a confederate of hers) enrolled in the courses under an assumed name and kept notes documenting work done, grades, contacts with the schools, and achievements. Woodyard reported on correspondence courses in nursing, crime detection, civil service, industrial management, advertising, radio repair, drawing, etiquette, French, and English.

Her chapter "Mastering English Usage" reports on Cody's course, though she does not mention it by name. Woodyard wrote to Cody's Rochester school assuming the identity of a middle-aged women embarrassed by her lack of education. When she asked whether she could "keep up with the class," she was told that if she had finished the sixth grade, she should be able to complete the work successfully. Overall Woodyard rated Cody's course as good. She thought that Cody's time schedule of 15 minutes a day was reasonable—she was able to complete the lessons in about five minutes and a Nutshell book in about 40 minutes. She also found the course material well organized and the method "as good as could be devised for the self correction of errors." The main problem, she wrote, was that the content was "often trivial, sometimes debatable as to its correctness, and too frequently out of date in its rulings." Woodyard suggested that with conscientious revision and proofing "there would be little fault to find with the course," thought she also noted that public libraries offered the same information at no cost.[12]

Woodyard's book provided an independent assessment of the strong points and the deficiencies of Cody's course. More generally, her study reflected the evolving and conflicted attitudes about private correspondence schools. Woodyard spoke favorably about the anonymity of correspondence education in which "the paper alone is scored, not the paper of the school hero nor the paper of its glamour girl."[13] She also found correspondence education useful for its flexibility of time, for providing a method of on-the-job training, and for helping to productively structure leisure time. On the other hand, she reported that all of the courses she examined over-advertised the ease of instruction, the benefits, and the degree of learning that could be obtained. She wondered, facetiously, why a course was needed at all if the knowledge is so easy to obtain, but she chided consumers as well by adding that "schools that promise more than they perform would find it hard to thrive in a country where no one wanted to get rich quick or to pass for more than he was worth in his job or in society."[14]

Woodyard's observations highlight the fundamental double nature of self-improvement courses like Cody's. Advertisements promised to raise people's financial and social status by focusing on appearances and impressions. But in promising the appearance and impression of an elite education in just minutes of self-study a day, such courses also subverted the value of those appearances and impressions. If the essentials of an elite education could be obtained for 30 dollars, was such an education really important?

Cody thought that it was, and the contrast between his advertising and his course suggests that he recognized this fundamental problem in his approach. He saw the work on appearances and impressions as the starting point to learning, rather than the endpoint, and he saw the 15 minutes a day as developing habits of learning rather than a mere shortcut. Like Charles Eliot and Dale Carnegie, he was offering a product that was transformational—that he hoped would lead to a long-term engagement with significant ideas. It is no small irony that the first impression Cody made on consumers was often grounded in the narrative of first impressions. But before Cody could introduce his larger ideas and new literary art, it was necessary to market the courses, and to do that the focus had to be on practical concerns. It is not so different for today's colleges and universities, which must blend an interest in the vocational with their commitment to the liberal arts. In many areas, we advertise impression management and practical skills but are really hoping to provide something more.

FIFTEEN

School's Out

IN THE 1920S AND 1930S, CODY'S WEALTH GREW. He continued to write and publish, working from his home in Dobbs Ferry, New York, where he became a leading citizen. Cody enjoyed a good life, and he and Marian found time for the arts, including classical music and both Broadway and local theatre.[1] The Codys were able to vacation and travel as well. They bought a summer home in upstate New York and visited Europe by ocean liner on several occasions. For a time, Cody continued to promote the National Ability Tests with articles in *Forbes* and other magazines, and he published books related to the tests, including *Standard Test English,* which appeared in 1920, and *Sherwin Cody's Business Ability Development Course,* released in 1923.[2] But eventually he put that work aside. Cody also returned to his interest in Edgar Allan Poe, reworking his introduction to Poe's tales and publishing an anthology titled *Poe—Man, Poet, and Creative Thinker* in 1924, though the book was not well received.[3]

During the 1930s, Cody became very involved in real estate development. When he and Marian decided to move to Dobbs Ferry, Cody bought a large tract of land there in 1928, near what is now the Saw Mill River Parkway, and the area was subdivided into home sites. Reporting on a unique home design in 1934 and later on the appointment of an official architect to the development, *The New York Times* referred to the area as "Sherwin Cody's Hilltop Park Community." Cody's 1950 entry in *Who's Who in America* described it as "Hilltop Park, a community for college profs."[4] Cody may have been intending a planned community of academics, but the project never came to fruition, and Cody sold the Hilltop Park land in the 1950s.

Much of Cody's time and energy, of course, was still devoted to writing and publishing his educational materials. Cody arranged for translations of his books into Spanish, French, German, and other languages. In the 1930s, he updated his 1903 series as *The New Art of Writing and Speaking the English Language,* publishing it in a single volume with new introductory material and with updated discussions of some topics.[5] Cody also revised his course in the 1930s. The 1936 revision of the course retained most of the 1918 material but had a number of changes. The revision included extra pages in each Tuesday lesson on pronunciation, with additional discussion of silent letters, exercises on finding the accent (word stress), and more exercises in identifying vowel length. The Friday lessons on Conversation and Reading were renamed Reading and Vocabulary, and the literary discussion of the earlier version was condensed by about half. This allowed more space in each booklet for vocabulary-building exercises. Some of these asked readers to identify synonyms for such words as *thrilling, glabrous, allay, enervating, stilted, scurrilous, peremptory, refulgent, polyglot,* and *retracted.*[6] Others provided new stylistic advice, cautioning students against awkward repetition (such as *We got up early and got breakfast*) and reminding them to find substitutes for overused "pet words," such as *nice, lovely,* and *funny.*[7] Cody added writing exercises in which students updated literary examples to modern style, a favorite technique of his. There was a new discussion of etymology in the 1936 edition, including suggestions about the use of Latin and Anglo-Saxon words for variety. Cody also expanded the material on the pronunciation of foreign words, perhaps reflecting his continued travels, the increased internationalism of the

1930s, and the role of radio in making the spoken word more prominent.

In several lessons the opening essays on rhetoric in the 1936 version are identical to those of the 1918 version. But others are more concise and show signs of revision and tightening. Lesson 3 on "How to Get Rid of Self-Consciousness," for example, condenses to two paragraphs what was a full page in the 1918 version, while at the same time broadening the discussion to include self-consciousness in conversation as well as writing. The first lesson of the 1936 course was also revised to ask readers to conduct a self-evaluation by answering the following questions:[8]

> Is your education up to your personal qualities, or do you have more talents than your education enables you to show up to advantage?
> Is your general personality attractive, just average, or rather negative?
> What sort of voice have you? . . .
> Have you a manner that is pleasant and attractive? Or do you incline to be silent?
> How much work are you willing to do to improve your weak points?

In all, the 1936 discussion of rhetoric and conversation was less literary and less introspective than the 1918 version had been. Cody's advice became more modern and struck many of the same themes as Dale Carnegie's did, encouraging attention to emotional and affective interactions. Lesson 1, for example, noted that "Success in language is fifty percent a matter of knowing your man or woman," and Lesson 8 emphasized tact and the need to avoid "flat-footed, uncompromising statements about religion or any other subject that other people hold dear." Cody warned against "personal criticism in public," "disregard for people's feelings," and "too much talking about one's self and one's personal interests."[9] And he explained how to handle parties and "office forces" by taking a personal interest in employees and by being friendly.[10]

There were other updatings as well. Adolf Hitler is cited as having "an unstable emotional nature" and a poor "command of language." Cody comments that Hitler "won his position chiefly by talking with passionate intensity. His fiery words overcame all his handicaps. But it requires a sort of fanatic determination." In a lesson that had earlier mentioned only Woodrow Wilson, Cody added Franklin D. Roosevelt, who "spoke with a cultured distinction such as we expect from a President, but his easy conversational tone never failed him."[11] In Cody's view, Wilson and Roosevelt had the same effective mix of colloquial and refined speech as Lincoln did, and they joined him as models of speech. Despite the various changes and updatings, however, Cody's core opinions about usage continued to be evident. He still advised students to cultivate colloquial vocabularies for "conversations, letter writing, and business" and he dismissed pretentiousness, reminding readers that "all the old formal literary writing has gone by today."[12]

While Cody's views remained steady, his interests grew with the times, and he often searched for new markets and opportunities. In 1944, at the age of 75, Cody addressed parents in *Coaching Children in English*. In the first half of the book, Cody stressed to parents that English skills are fundamental for children's socialization and social mobility, and he once again emphasized the importance of colloquial English, reading, and letter writing.[13] He told parents that classroom drill on grammar "creates more confusions than it corrects," dismissed the practice of marking errors as largely ineffective, and suggested that academic writing resulted in "dull intellectual criticisms." Instead, he advocated a student-centered approach involving individual coaching and sequential activities that build interest in interacting with and making a good impression on "other well-educated children or adults."[14] The guided self-criticism he suggested was essentially a version of the self-correcting method of his correspondence course.[15] By 1944, Cody's understanding of the importance of English skills had expanded in its goals as well. In his early works, the goal was to motivate vocationally minded students to master English for their own financial advancement and for the needs of business.[16] In *Coaching Children,* however, Cody seemed equally worried about the social consequences caused by inferiority complexes, of which "the English language is the principal source."[17] He wrote that:

> The schools are a great social grinding machine. Four million go into the hopper every year, and only two million graduate. What becomes of the other two million? Why, they are "retarded," they are branded as "too stupid to learn." They get an inferiority complex. They learn to hate their teachers. They begin to play truant. Before you know it they are in the juvenile courts—or someplace that is just about as bad.[18]

In *Coaching Children,* Cody also promoted Maria Montessori's ideas at a time when interest in her approach had waned in the United States. Montessori's principles, first elaborated in 1912, involved children working at their own pace, often with imaginative, self-directed, and self-correcting materials. As biographer Rita Kramer notes, Montessori often told teachers that "When you have solved the problem of controlling the attention of the child, you have solved the entire problem of education."[19] Cody, whose ads sometimes stressed making learning like a game, agreed that English was an "unconscious art." But he also thought that English instruction "must be carefully organized so that emphasis is placed upon the confusions and difficulties of our language, so that explanations are easily at hand, and so that the whole subject can be handled in the normal childish rhythms."[20] He advocated a naturalistic method of learning English at the elementary level—through reading, storytelling, letter writing, and other activities—but insisted that attention be paid to the 100 confusing points of usage, to the 250 troublesome words, and to the handful of principles of form and punctuation "necessary to give the appearance of 'literacy' to a child's letters and composition papers."[21] The teaching material presented in the appendix to *Coaching Children* was intended to facilitate this natural method, and Cody described it as fun, fast-paced, and scientifically tested.[22]

Cody continued working through his seventies and eighties. In the 1940s he began preparing a series of picture books to teach English to speakers of other languages and to help non-natives understand the differences between British and American usage. Cody had gotten interested in the linguistic work of British writer C. K. Ogden, whose Basic English was an attempt to simplify the language and create a universal international English that would be easy to learn. The simplest version of Basic English included just 850 words—mostly nouns and words which could be taught through pictures—plus a small set of simplified rules of grammar. Odgen explained that

> Basic English is . . . a language of eight hundred and fifty English words which will say clearly and simply almost everything we normally say with fifteen or twenty thousand. . . . Basic is less concerned to alter the way we speak than to encourage a different attitude to what we say. For the foreigner it provides a means of communication which will be indistinguishable from Standard English; to the English-speaking peoples it offers an educational instrument by which contexts and connections can be analyzed in the interests of a fuller appreciation of the resources of the language as a whole.[23]

In a series of letters to Ogden in 1943 and 1944, Cody proposed a collaboration in which he would use Basic English and promote it in his new course on English for non-native speakers. Cody's proposed *English Self-Taught Through Story of Life in America* would include pictures of scenes he thought would be familiar to immigrants (a dock, customs, a baggage porter, a taxi, etc.) along with exercises and vocabulary keyed to those settings. Explaining his idea to Ogden, Cody noted that while his *100%*

Self-correcting Course was a great success, it required a fifth-grade education and was thus unsuitable for the "20,000,000 near illiterates we have in America, as well as people in Russia, China, etc."[24] Cody and Ogden were never able to come to agreement, Ogden apparently fearing that Cody wished to trade on the notoriety of Basic English. But Cody got far enough along on the project to request permission from the U.S. Treasury to picture currency in the book. Cody's letters to Ogden grew increasing chilly (their salutations going from *Dear Sir* to *Dear Dr. Ogden* to *Dear Professor Ogden* to *Dear Mr. Ogden*) and Cody at one point added a postscript that "No one has a mortgage on the English language."[25]

Cody's final publication seems to have been a letter to the *New York Times* in 1952, disagreeing with a review of Cornelia Otis Skinner's one-woman show "Paris '90." Cody wrote that Skinner's play provided characterizations that were "quite in the same class with the drawings of Toulouse-Lautrec and the other great artists who have pictured the women of Paris."[26] Despite his age, he was still planning book projects in the 1950s. In 1956 he wrote to Alfred Knopf about a book he was planning on writing styles. Explaining that he lacked American examples, Cody asked if there might be a short selection of H. L. Mencken's that would be interesting to contemporary readers.[27] Neither of his last planned projects saw publication, however. Cody suffered a stroke in 1957 and moved to the home of his friend and caretaker, Nellie Brink, in Brooklyn, New York. He passed away two years later in the Woods Nursing Home on April 4, 1959, at the age of 90.

SERIOUS, HARD-WORKING, INDEFATIGABLE

In the early part of the twentieth century, Cody launched a humor magazine called *The Touchstone*. It lasted only five issues and may simply have been the wrong genre for his talents. By many accounts, including his own, he had a serious, Victorian character. He started work at a young age due to his economic and family circumstances, and he was driven by his promise to his mother, by his outsider social status at Amherst, and by the rejection of the literary friends who thought his turn to business made him a philistine. Cody became both a habitual entrepreneur and workaholic. Even on vacations, he focused on business. When the family visited Italy in 1910, Cody immersed himself in the study of Italian, and he spent time arranging for translations of his books on letter writing. His grandson, Peter Malcolm Cody, recalls that on family outings Sherwin would bring along a portable typewriter in his Packard (he purchased a new Packard every few years) and would sit in the woods working at his books. Peter Cody remembers his grandfather as something of a curmudgeon who occasionally emerged from his study to take him for a walk, although he notes that Sherwin did seem to mellow as he grew older.

A measure of Cody's nineteenth-century reserve is that he never mentioned Marian by name in his books and had relatively little to say about her in his running autobiography. For their time, the Codys had an unusual marriage. They kept separate finances, and Marian often traveled back to her native England by herself. In a 1981 reminiscence, the Codys' son Morrill wrote that Sherwin had promised her an opportunity to visit home every few years, and that Morrill and his mother spent half-years in England on several occasions. Marian had a literary background herself, and Morrill reported to Carter Daniel that she was the actual writer of most of the poetry anthology that Cody published at the turn of the century.[28]

Sherwin Cody seems to have been a distant parent. Morrill was educated largely at boarding schools in France and in Indiana, and he recalled once traveling back to New York from England alone during World War I. His father was supposed to meet him at the docks, but arranged instead for Morrill to be picked up by a friend. The friend never arrived, and it was left to a priest to arrange for Morrill to catch the train to Illinois.[29] Carter Daniel reports that Morrill admired his father's great drive, but thought him boring and self-centered, and Morrill described his father to Daniel as puritanical, bigoted, and miserly. Daniel also notes that, in Morrill's view, Marian was often bored with Sherwin as well.[30] It is clear that Sherwin thought highly of his own talents,

Morrill Cody

In 1901 Sherwin and Marian Cody had their only child, a son named Edward Morrill Cody. Morrill, as he was known, was educated in Paris and at the Interlaken School, where he roomed with the nephew of Henry Ford and the future head of Sears Roebuck. He followed in his father's steps by attending Amherst College, graduating in 1921.

Morrill's early travels and foreign experience gave him a fluency in French that led to a career as a foreign correspondent, journalist (for *The Dial* and *Literary Digest*), and magazine editor in Paris in the 1920s and 1930s. From 1941 through 1976, he worked in the U.S. Foreign Service, serving in Paraguay, Argentina, Mexico, Washington, Paris, Stockholm, Madrid, and New York. During the Kennedy administration he was Deputy Director of the U.S. Information Agency, where he worked under Edward R. Murrow. He ended his career in Paris as bureau manager for Radio Liberty from 1965 to 1976.

Morrill Cody was an amateur painter with a lifelong interest in art and literature. He wrote or cowrote four books about France: *This Must Be the Place,* the reminiscences of a famous barman, James Charters (later published as *Hemingway's Paris*); *The Women of Montparnasse; The Favorite Restaurants of an American in Paris;* and *Passing Stranger,* a novel. He was also acquainted with the Paris-based writers and artists of the day, including Hemingway, the Fitzgeralds, Dali, Duchamp, Ezra Pound, Man Ray, Djuna Barnes, Isadora Duncan, Ford Madox Ford, Gertrude Stein, Alice B. Toklas, and Sylvia Beach. Morrill Cody was married four times, to Frances Ryan, Marian Holbrook, Verna Feurheim, and Jane Hoster, and had three children, Peter Malcolm Cody, Judith Alden Cody Kirk, and Gabrielle Hamilton Cody.

importance, and personal mission as an educator—even to the extent of including his own life story in a practical course on grammar. He seems to have had a negative view of the average person's intelligence, but he was nevertheless utopian in many ways and confident of the ability of applied science to improve life for the great mass of people. Working essentially nonstop from the time his mother died in 1880 until his stroke in 1957 and publishing over 200 articles and books, he was, as *The Nation* called him in a 1918 book notice, "indefatigable."[31]

MAYBE YOUSE DON'T TALK LIKE THIS

The Sherwin Cody School of English struggled in the 1950s as the cost of ads began to outstrip the revenue from the course. With the retirement of Walter Paterson and Charles Lennon in 1953, Cody closed the Rochester office. He transferred the franchise to George Kemp's U.S. School of Music, and the school was sold again after Cody's death.[32] His long-running advertising campaign in *The New York Times* ended in December of 1959, although ads for *The Art of Writing and Speaking the English Language* continued in comic books into the 1960s.

Why did the Cody course falter in the 1950s? One factor, naturally, was Cody's advanced age and failing health. But there is more to the end of the Sherwin Cody School than simply a business venture that failed to outlive its founder. In a way, the school suffered from its own success, doing well enough for so long that no changes were made in the basic business model until it was too late. Perhaps if Cody had organized his school differently to establish local franchises or other enterprises, things might have turned out differently. The International Correspondence Schools and the Alexander Hamilton Institute reinvented themselves over the years to find new niches, and self-improvement products like Charles Atlas's Dynamic-Tension and Dale Carnegie Training have remained strong. The Carnegie course, for example, evolved from an emphasis on interpersonal skills, likeability, and happiness to an international training program that offers courses and seminars in organizational development, change management, sales, team building, and executive leadership. By expanding its focus from individuals to organizations as made up of individuals, the Carnegie organization has proved durable in the marketplace. Dale Carnegie's franchise system was also certainly a factor in the long-term success of his courses. Equally important was the role that Carnegie's widow Dorothy played after his death in 1955, leading the business for the next four decades. Today Dale Carnegie Training offers programs in 70 countries and in more than 25 languages, and over seven million people have completed a Carnegie course or seminar.[33] Cody, however, did not have a natural successor to manage his course into the second half of the twentieth century. Marian Cody had passed away in 1943, and Morrill had his own literary interests and career in the U.S. Foreign Service. The main collaborators for Cody's school, other than Walter Paterson and Charles Lennon, were Schwab and Beatty. But Schwab and Beatty were also approaching retirement after many years in the ad business.[34]

By 1950 Cody's ad had run for over 30 years, mostly with the same picture of the middle-aged Cody—which Morrill described as being as familiar as the Smith Brothers whose faces decorated boxes of cough drops. For all those years, the marketing message remained essentially static—explaining why people made mistakes, extolling Cody's work in the Gary, Indiana, schools, and promising a self-correcting device. The advertising campaign may simply have become so familiar to readers that it was easily skipped over. Also, by the 1950s, the context of Cody's ad had become that of an increasingly skeptical popular culture, and the ad was satirized in the newly founded *Mad* magazine with a parody that asked "Do People Laugh at You for Reading Comic Books?"[35] Schwab and Beatty would even poke fun at it themselves in a 1957 *New York*

Times advertisement. The standard body of the Cody ad was used, but with a new headline that read "Maybe youse don't talk like this, but—." The ad did not turn the fortunes of the course around, though it did stimulate a mocking critique in the trade magazine *Advertising Age*. The columnist writing the Creative Man's Corner wrote that Cody had erred in abandoning his famous caption because the phrase "Maybe youse don't talk like this" was "certainly not addressed to us and, in our opinion, the person who does actually say 'yuce' (or 'yous') would be too insulted to read the thing." The *Advertising Age* column in turn elicited a reply by George Kemp of the U.S. School of Music, who noted that the *youse* ad actually had a higher immediate response than the old standard.[36] It was, however, too late for new advertising to reverse the fortunes of the *100% Self-correcting Course*.

Cody's static business model, the lack of a succession plan, and the staleness of his ads were probably not the only factors in the decline of the *100% Self-correcting Course*. When the course was sold a final time after Cody's death, George Kemp suggested that "The correspondence courses used to be popular among people who wanted to advance themselves and speak better. Now no one cares about grammatical errors."[37] Kemp was not the only one suggesting a public indifference toward good grammar. Historian Jacques Barzun was drawing the attention of intellectuals to a supposed decline in grammar and culture. Barzun had been featured on the cover of *Time* magazine in 1956 and became provost and dean of the Columbia University faculty in 1958, so he had some measure of authority as an advocate of linguistic propriety.[38]

Kemp may have assumed that radio and television were subverting grammatical correctness by emphasizing the spoken language over the literary standard. Television and radio did in fact help to promote colloquial usage in entertainment programs and commercials. For example, the television program *Who Do You Trust?* involved host Johnny Carson speaking to real people, and the show promoted itself by flaunting the supposed incorrectness

The Creative Man's Corner . . .

How Do Youse Feel About It?

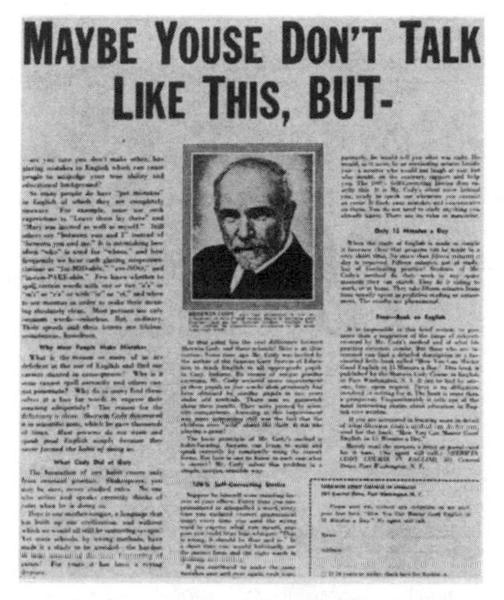

MAYBE YOUSE DON'T TALK LIKE THIS, BUT-

When we saw this ad we were, frankly, shocked to find how much Sherwin Cody had aged. But we were even more shocked to discover how, after having for years tried to sell people on avoiding common mistakes in English, he has at long last succumbed to the vulgate and speaks, these days, like a Dead End Kid—"Maybe Youse Don't Talk Like Tthis, But—"

We may as well admit that we immediately found ourselves wondering who decided that *Yous* is spelt *Youse*. Was it Mr. Cody? And how does he justify the inclusion of the "e?" *Louse* is pronounced "laus" or "lowce." *Youse* is, therefore, hardly pronounced "yuce." It is, rather, pronounced "yowce."

For years we wondered how Mr. Cody could be so confident that "Shakespeare . . . never studied rules." Seeing his current photo, we wonder no longer.

Anyway, we think Mr. Cody has made a mistake abandoning not just the photo he has used for years, but the caption—the one about making those common mistakes in English. This caption is a phony caption. It is certainly not addressed to us and, in our opinion, the person who does actually say "yuce" (or "yous") would be too insulted to read the thing.

By the way, Sher—were you related to Bill? #

FIGURE 15.1. Reaction to the Youse ad (reprinted with permission from the April 14, 1958, issue of *Advertising Age*, Copyright, Crain Communications, Inc., 1958).

of its grammar. Advertisers used colloquial speech in such slogans as "Winston tastes good—like a cigarette should." As the "Maybe youse don't talk like this" advertisement suggested, bad grammar was becoming good advertising. But at the same time, the broadcast media relied on manuals like the *NBC Handbook of Pronunciation,* just as the print media relied on house style guides for written usage.[39] And high schools, colleges, and universities continued to teach grammar and usage, even as they experimented with new approaches.

Social and market changes probably had a greater effect on the decline of the *100% Self-correcting Course* than did attitudes about English. The rise of television was changing the advertising market. Television competed with pulp magazines and newspapers for consumers' attention, and the natural constituency for Cody's message—the working-class and middle-class reader—was turning to new forms of mass media. The pulps drastically lost circulation in the mid-forties as production costs and competition increased, and Sunday newspaper circulation, which had grown significantly from 1920 to 1950, also began to flatten.[40]

New demographics of education and new competition within the education market were also factors. Adjusting to criticisms and legal controls, private correspondence schools survived the depression and World War II, and in the postwar era began providing consumers with more and more comprehensive offerings. According to the National Home Study Council, correspondence schools were still a $50,000,000 business in 1961, and *The New York Times* estimated that 1,500,000 students were enrolled in commercial correspondence work that year.[41] As the correspondence school industry grew, Cody's piece of it faced ever-increasing competition.

Universities were competing better as well. After World War II, the Servicemen's Readjustment Act of 1944 (the "GI Bill of Rights") provided tuition for veterans to attend colleges and universities, and by 1946 more than one million veterans enrolled in college through the GI Bill. Many veterans choose correspondence schools, but traditional colleges also established special programs to attract veterans. As a diverse group of veterans entered higher education, there was a renewed interest in basic English skills in colleges and universities. And higher education would expand for many years, accommodating not just the returning servicemen but, after a brief lull, the first wave of the baby boomers and the Vietnam generation. As these ever larger pools of students entered universities, the attention to practical English education remained intense.

For the Sherwin Cody course, there was increasing competition from all sides. Private correspondence schools were offering English, accounting, and even law. Colleges and universities were reaching out to broader student populations, and new practical grammar books were entering the market. And as tastes continued to change in language and culture, Cody's course on English and reading, largely unchanged since 1918, must have seemed increasingly dated. By the time of the 1969 moon landing, ten years after Cody's death, the phrase "Do You Make These Mistakes in Grammar?" was already a bit of history.

SIXTEEN

The Sherwin Cody Legacy

SUCCESSFUL ENTREPRENEURS HAVE AN UNDERSTANDing of the direction of a culture and the needs of a society, they create things that address those needs, and they understand how to communicate their ideas in mass markets. Sherwin Cody was such a person. Like many entrepreneurs, he worked across boundaries—across the boundaries of business, grammar, literature, testing, self-education, publishing, and advertising. Cody was not always the originator of new ideas, but he had the great skill of pioneering and marketing them. From his early experiences with the typewriter and the hectograph to his final idea of using pictures to teach non-native speakers, Cody was often at the leading edge of changes that have today become part of the norm.

As a way of taking stock of Cody's contributions, it helps to sort them into business and educational innovations, although the two categories often overlap. His business efforts included ventures in publishing, marketing, and advertising psychology. When lower-cost postage established mail-order advertising and bulk correspondence as a new marketing technology, Cody made this the center of his business activities. Always mindful of efficiency, he was a great recycler of material and reissued parts of his works in many different combinations. Cody also understood the connection of narrative literature to applied psychology and of applied psychology to sales practices. As an advertiser and consultant, he promoted the formula of Attention, Interest, Desire, and Action, and as a mail-order businessman himself, he advocated putting attention on the customer rather than the manufacturer. His "scientific approach" to business involved tracking the results of ad campaigns to provide correction and to improve sales. And he was an experimenter, trying new techniques like the negative option, an innovation in mail order later made famous by the Book-of-the-Month Club.

As an educator, Cody's emphasis was on the vocational and nontraditional student, and as an education critic it was on the failure of the schools and the limitations of formal literary conventions. Working without an institutional home or disciplinary affiliation, Cody was an early advocate of using the colloquial language in business and business education. Today the colloquial—simple, conversational, and direct language—is accepted as the standard by most of the knowledgeable educational establishment and by publishers. In the early 1900s, however, this was still in many ways a controversial view, especially among English educators.

Cody also helped to define vocational English education with letter writing as the pedagogical bridge between speaking and writing. If he were alive today, he would doubtless be focusing on the relation between spoken language and electronic mail. He was a relentless critic of "unscientific" composition pedagogy, and he disliked both traditional grading methods and laissez-faire progressive ones, favoring guided self-correction. As a critic of university education, Cody faulted liberal arts curricula based on the classics and on passive recitation of theory and definition. And while Cody did not have the impact of others, he was among the early adopters of aptitude testing and outcomes assessment, connecting these developments to business progressivism and meritocracy. In Cody's view, efficiency, testing, and incentives would together provide a rising standard of living for those willing to put in effort.[1]

Cody also advocated student-centered education that motivated and interested students. He sought to make study less time-consuming, less tedious, and less dull—more like a game or athletic contest—so that the average person would enjoy learning. Even as he encouraged his students to approach self-education in a businesslike fashion, committing daily time to improvement, he also understood the need for learning to be pleasant. Enjoyment was the key to lifelong self-improvement.

CORRECTING YOUR SELF

Sherwin Cody's background had convinced him that one's worth was determined by aptitude, work, and reliability rather than by the circumstances of birth, and he thought that anyone's life would improve through self-study. Cody committed himself to making this possible, and his work was influential to the readers of his dozens of books, to his 150,000-plus correspondence students, and to the fields of business communication, English education, and advertising. However, he did not have the impact of a John Franklin Genung, Sterling Leonard, Charles Eliot, or Dale Carnegie, receiving scant mention in the fields of testing, psychology, English linguistics, or literature. Still, his is an important story in many ways.

The story of Sherwin Cody and the *100% Self-correcting Course* is about how impressions—in this case, impressions created by language—matter. The durability of his famous advertisement and the success of his course testify to the power of grammar anxiety and the durability of the success and self-improvement narrative. At the core of this narrative is the belief that language education teaches conduct, manages impressions, instills self-confidence, and helps us find happiness. The management of linguistic impressions remains with us today, though it is addressed in ways other than correspondence courses: we find it in middle school and high school English classes, in college composition courses, and in practical handbooks, remedial workbooks, test preparation courses, business grammar seminars, grammar web sites, and accent reduction courses.[2] And of course other types of instruction in conduct, self-confidence, success, and happiness are with us as well. Today we still attempt to avoid anxiety and achieve fulfillment through new generations of products and self-help activities.

Sherwin Cody's story is also a story about the democratization of language. The *100% Self-correcting Course* succeeded for so many years by defining good English in practical ways, with instruction that was more down-to-earth and practical than school textbooks of the same period. Cody understood and embraced the average person's interest in knowing the standards and rules signifying social class—the telling "mistakes" by which potential is judged. At the same time, he encouraged realism of another sort, reminding his students to attend not only to the standards of social class but also to the expectations of real listeners and real audiences. Language that was too pedantic, too formal, or too literary was just as wrong as language that was provincial, vulgar, or uneducated. To succeed in the world, people needed to pay attention not just to linguistic norms but to how their speech and writing was perceived by others. In helping his students to understand language in this way, Cody recognized and promoted the idea that the twentieth century was becoming a new social, linguistic, and educational frontier in which good English belonged to its speakers.

Finally, Sherwin Cody's story is about what it means to succeed. Cody's modern view of correctness held that good language was colloquial and that norms were relative, but Cody did not see people as mere linguistic chameleons. He encouraged his students to develop taste by conversation and reading and to improve their inner lives by engaging with high culture. In this, Cody's work reminds us of how self-improvement brings together opposites, treating culture and language as tools for impression-management and also as tools for fulfillment and self-growth. Everyone wanted a measure of security, respect, success, and happiness, Cody believed, and ongoing self-study was the key to making that happen. The real Cody legacy may not be in the grammatical work, the business-like approach, the clever advertising, or the literary recommendations, but in how he guided individuals to take responsibility for their own education through ongoing study and reading. We know Sherwin Cody first from his signature question—"Do You Make These Mistakes in English?" But we should understand him in terms of the title of his course—*The 100% Self-correcting Course in English Language*. It was a course about correcting the self.

Notes

Chapter One

1. Julian Lewis Watkins included it in his 1949 book *The 100 Greatest Advertisements,* and a panel of 97 advertising professionals placed it in the bicentennial collection of 200 top ads. See Julian Lewis Watkins, *The 100 Greatest Advertisements: Who Wrote Them and What They Did* (New York: Moore, 1949; rev. ed. New York: Dover, 1959), 68–69; Frank Rowsome, Jr., *They Laughed When I Sat Down: An Informal History of Advertising in Words and Pictures* (New York: Bonanza Books, 1959), 152–155; editors of *Advertising Age, How It Was in Advertising: 1776–1976* (Chicago: Crain Books, 1976), 46. A Cody ad was mentioned as early as 1929 in the unpaginated Illustrated Appendix to Frank Presbrey's *The History and Development of Advertising* (Garden City, NY: Doubleday, Doran, 1929).
2. In Lesson 15, Cody explains that "the past tense indicates time wholly past." Sherwin Cody, *100% Self-correcting Course in English Language* (Rochester, NY: Sherwin Cody School of English, 1918), 15, 7.
3. See page 42 for an example of a longer ad.

Chapter Two

1. Cody, *100% Self-correcting Course*, Lesson 2, 2. The course included a running autobiography of Cody's first 50 years, and Cody notes that his paternal great-grandfather had had 11 children, one of whom was Buffalo Bill Cody's father.

2. Cody, *100% Self-correcting Course*, Lesson 6, 2.
3. Cody, *100% Self-correcting Course*, Lesson 11, 2. Cody reflected that he would have had more opportunity to earn money attending college in Cambridge, Massachusetts, than in Amherst.
4. Cody, *100% Self-correcting Course*, Lesson 12, 2.
5. Cody, *100% Self-correcting Course*, Lesson 14, 2.
6. Cody, *100% Self-correcting Course*, Lesson 14, 2. Cody recognized that the classical perspective was important because "The practical things one learns in any school are usually quite out of date when the time comes for one to use them."
7. Cody, *100% Self-correcting Course*, Lesson 14, 2.
8. Sherwin Cody, *Good English Form Book in Business Letter Writing* (Chicago: School of English, 1904), 25. Cody reproduces a sample job application letter he sent to Marshall Fields outlining his work history after college. The interview with Holmes was from the Dec. 19, 1891, issue of the *Chicago Tribune* and is reported on in "Holmes Interview Presented to School," *Chicago Daily Herald,* Nov. 11, 1966.
9. Cody, *100% Self-correcting Course*, Lesson 17, 2.
10. Sherwin Cody, *The Art of Writing and Speaking the English Language: Constructive Rhetoric* (G. P. Putnam's Sons, 1922), 11, 22, 30.
11. Cody, *Constructive Rhetoric,* 24–25.
12. According to Cody, the book arose when a reader of his newspaper writing contacted him to study story writing, apparently by correspondence. Cody described the book as the first of its kind.
13. Sherwin Cody, *In the Heart of the Hills* (London: J. M. Dent, 1896), 294. Later Cody arranged for the book to be serialized in some American newspapers.
14. Cody, *100% Self-correcting Course*, Lesson 17, 2.
15. Sherwin Cody, *The New Art of Writing and Speaking the English Language,* 1938, 331–32.
16. Cody, *100% Self-correcting Course*, Lesson 20, 2.
17. Cody, *100% Self-correcting Course*, Lesson 20, 2.
18. Cody, *100% Self-correcting Course*, Lesson 20, 2.
19. "New humorous magazine," *New York Times Book Review,* Dec. 16, 1905, 899.

Chapter Three

1. Francis Weeks, "The Teaching of Business Writing at the Collegiate Level, 1900–1920," in *Studies in the History of Business Writing,* ed. George

H. Douglas and Herbert W. Hildebrandt (Urbana, Ill.: Association for Business Communication, 1985), 204.

2. As historian Arthur M. Schlesinger has noted, works like W. H. Dilworth's *The Complete Letter-Writer* were popular even in the late eighteenth century as part of the training of newly prosperous merchants and tradesmen: *Learning How to Behave: A Historical Study of American Etiquette Books* (New York: Macmillan, 1946), 9.
3. Cody, *The Art of Writing and Speaking the English Language,* vol. IV, *Constructive Rhetoric* (Chicago: The Old Greek Press, 1903), 13.
4. See Joseph M. Williams, *Style: Toward Clarity and Grace* (Chicago: University of Chicago, 1990) and William Zinsser, *On Writing Well,* 5th ed. (New York: Harper Collins, 1995).
5. Sherwin Cody, *How to Do Business by Letter,* 62 (Chicago: School of English, 1908).
6. Cody, *Constructive Rhetoric,* 11.
7. Cody, *How to Do Business by Letter,* 7.
8. J. Willis Westlake, *How to Write Letters: A Manual of Correspondence, Showing the Correct Structure, Composition, Punctuation, Formalities, and Uses of the Various Kinds of Letters, Notes, and Cards* (Philadelphia: Sower, Potts, 1876). John Hagge, a historian of business communication, emphasizes Westlake's role in "The Spurious Paternity of Business Communication Principles," *Journal of Business Communication* 26(1989): 33–55. More broadly, Hagge sees modern techniques of business communication not as new ideas but as reinventions of rhetorical notions that can be traced to the Greeks.
9. Weeks, "The Teaching of Business Writing," 202. Hotchkiss included the idea of "character," which covered both politeness and friendliness. In 1916 Hotchkiss developed a college textbook, *Business English, Its Principles and Practice,* coauthored with Celia Anne Drew (New York: The American Book Company).
10. Edwin H, Lewis, *A First Book in Writing English* (New York: Macmillan & Co, 1898). According to Weeks, the Alexander Hamilton Institute and the A. W. Shaw Company also issued early books for home study in letter writing.
11. Carter Daniel, "Sherwin Cody: Business Communication Pioneer," *Journal of Business Communication* 19(1982): 3–14.
12. See William H. Burnham, "Principles of Municipal School Management," *The Atlantic Monthly* 92(1903): 105–09, and Raymond E. Callahan, *Education and the Cult of Efficiency* (Chicago: University of Chicago Press, 1962), 10.
13. See Cody's *Business Practices Up to Date: Or How to Be a Private Secretary* (Chicago: School of English, 1913), 159. Cody also cites Frank Gilbreth and Harrington Emerson as leaders in the scientific management movement

and Arthur Frederick Sheldon and Walter Dill Scott as influences in personal salesmanship and advertising, respectively.

14. Sherwin Cody, "Scientific Principles in the Teaching of Composition," *English Journal* 1(1912): 164.
15. Cody, "Scientific Principles," 163–64.
16. Cody, "Scientific Principles," 168. He followed up in *English Journal* with a two-part article in 1914 on "The Ideal Course in English for Vocational Students," *English Journal* 3(1914): 263–81 and 371–80, continued in 1917 with "Organizing Drill on Fundamentals Like a Football Game," *English Journal* 6(1917): 412–19.
17. Sherwin Cody, *Coaching Children in English* (New York: Good English Publishers, 1944), 11.
18. The movement of students from room to room for different activities and studies led to this sometimes being known as the "platoon system." Today the Gary senior high school is the William A. Wirt School.
19. William Wirt, "Scientific Management of School Plants," *American School Board Journal* 42(1911): 2.
20. John and Evelyn Dewey, *Schools of Tomorrow* (New York: E.P. Dutton & Co., 1915), 175–204, 252–69.
21. Callahan, *Education and the Cult of Efficiency,* 136–38.
22. Cody, *100% Self-correcting Course*, Lesson 23, 2.
23. "Opening the Door to the Employee: An Effort at Co-operation to Put Commercial Education on a Better Basis," *New York Times,* April 11, 1915.
24. Sherwin Cody, *Commercial Tests and How to Use Them* (Yonkers-on-Hudson, NY: World Book Company, 1919), 12.
25. Cody, *Commercial Tests,* 20.
26. Cody, *Commercial Tests,* 208.
27. Sherwin Cody, *Standard Test English*. New York: Association Press [YMCA], 1920.
28. Cody, *Commercial Tests*, 2.
29. Cody, *Commercial Tests*, 8.
30. Cody, *Commercial Tests*, 6.
31. Cody, *Commercial Tests*, 20.

Chapter Four

1. Robert R. Doane, *The Measurement of American Wealth* (New York: Harper and Brothers, 1933), 10–11, cited by Schlesinger, 83. According to Doane, wealth rose from $30,400,000,000 to $126,700,000,000 from 1870 to 1900 and to $254,200,000,000 by 1914.

2. Ellen Gruber Garvey, *The Adman in the Parlor: Magazines and the Gendering of Consumer Culture, 1880s to 1910s* (New York: Oxford University Press, 1996), 56.
3. Barton, Bruce, *The Man Nobody Knows* (Indianapolis: Bobbs-Merrill, 1925). For a recent assessment, see John Ramage, *Twentieth-Century American Success Rhetoric: How to Construct a Suitable Self*, chap. 2 (Carbondale: Southern Illinois University Press, 2005).
4. Calvin Coolidge, "The Economic Aspects of Advertising" (reprinted in Presbrey, *History and Development of Advertising*, 620).
5. Roland Marchand, *Advertising and the American Dream: Making Way for Modernity, 1920–1940* (Berkeley: University of California Press, 1985), 27.
6. Maxwell Sackheim, *My First Sixty Years in Advertising* (Englewood Cliffs, N.J.: Prentice Hall, 1970), 80.
7. Sackheim himself noted the ad's use of the patent medicine formula in creating a disease out of relatively innocuous symptoms and then offering a cure. *My First Sixty Years*, 80.
8. Sherwin Cody, *How to Deal with Human Nature in Business* (Chicago: School of English, 1915), 199.
9. By coding the reply coupons, copywriters meticulously tracked the response rates from different version of ads and from different placements in magazines.
10. Victor O. Schwab, "An Advertisement That Is Never Changed," *Printers' Ink Monthly*, Sept. 1939, 10–11, 64–65.
11. John Caples, *Making Ads Pay* (New York: Dover Publications, 1966, reprint of New York: Harper and Brothers, 1957), 77–78. See also his *Tested Advertising Methods*, 4th ed. (Englewood Cliffs: Prentice Hall, 1984), 128.
12. "Which Ad Pulled Better?" *New York Times*, July 16, 1956.

Chapter Five

1. Sherwin Cody, *How You Can Master Good English—in 15 Minutes a Day* (Rochester, NY: Sherwin Cody School of English, 1929), 5.
2. Cody, *How You Can Master Good English*, 3, 4.
3. Cody, *How You Can Master Good English*, 4. A bit later he reminds readers that "Good English and good manners seem to go together in the minds of many people, and an offence on either score causes them such annoyance that they refuse to associate with people who violate the ethics of breeding" (ibid., 14).
4. Cody, *How You Can Master Good English*, 6–7, 14–15. Another example involved a man whose sales letters were correct but "colorless" but who increased the response rate by studying with Cody.

5. Cody, *How You Can Master Good English*, 6, 8, 17, 20. A sidebar explains that the course is designed for non-native speakers, grade school and high school dropouts, workers, businessmen, professionals, political activists, young men and women, wives, and parents. Testimonials were included from students and from English educators. Frederick H. Bair, a prominent school superintendent, wrote that the Cody system "deserves careful study on the part of school superintendents everywhere," and Ernest R. Clark, a well-known English educator in Rochester, added "I believe you have hit—as closely as it can be hit—the need of a student who has lost the opportunity for high school and college training" 26, 30.
6. Cody, *How You Can Master Good English*, 23.
7. Cody, *How You Can Master Good English*, 23.
8. Form letter from A. E. McCarthy, Supervisor of Study, dated June 12, 1924.
9. Cody, *100% Self-correcting Course*, Lesson 24, 2.
10. Cody, *100% Self-correcting Course*, Lesson 2, 3.
11. Cody, *Word Study* (*The Art of Writing and Speaking the English Language*, vol. I) (Chicago: The Old Greek Press, 1903), 29.
12. Cody, *The New Art of Writing and Speaking the English Language* (New York: The Sun Dial Press, 1938), 109. Cody also referred readers to Daniel Jones's *Pronouncing Dictionary for British English* and to George Philip Krapp's *Modern English*.
13. Cody, *100% Self-correcting Course*, Lesson 3, 3. As an example of a vowel whose length is determined by stress he gives *nā 'tion*. As an example of length determined by derivation he gives *hē ro' ic* from *hē' ro*.
14. Cody transcribes this difference inconsistently, using both *c* and *k* for *k* sounds (*kōrs* and *rek'omend,* but *comit'e* and *cordyuly*).
15. Cody, *100% Self-correcting Course*, Lesson 5, 3.
16. Cody, *100% Self-correcting Course*, Lesson 1, 4.
17. Cody, *100% Self-correcting Course*, Lessons 4, 4; 17, 4; 15, 4; and 13, 4.
18. Cody, *100% Self-correcting Course*, Lesson 20, 4.
19. Cody, *100% Self-correcting Course*, Lesson 21, 3; 19, 3.
20. Cody, *100% Self-correcting Course*, Lesson 22, 3.
21. Cody, *100% Self-correcting Course*, Lesson 22, 3.
22. Cody, *100% Self-correcting Course*, Lesson 15, 5. Dashes "indicates an abrupt transition—a positive stopping and then going ahead again, a break in the logical continuity of the sentence," and Cody perpetuates the idea that the overuse of dashes is feminine style, saying "Women in society almost have a fad for using dashes at the ends of sentences in place of periods."
23. Cody, *100% Self-correcting Course*, Lesson 20, 5.

24. Cody, *100% Self-correcting Course*, Lesson 19, 5.
25. Cody, *100% Self-correcting Course*, Lesson 4, 5.
26. Cody, *100% Self-correcting Course*, Lesson 6, 5.
27. Cody, *100% Self-correcting Course*, Lesson 7, 5. He does use the term "restrictive" in the answer key, however, but without defining it explicitly.
28. Cody, *New Art,* 1938, 81–2.
29. Cody, *New Art*, 1938, 75. Cody also suggested that the modern style was to leave commas out unless they were needed for contrast or emphasis.
30. Cody, *Brief Fundamentals* (Rochester: Sherwin Cody School of English, 1936), 33–36.

Chapter Six

1. Cody, *100% Self-correcting Course*, Lesson 1, 7.
2. Cody, *100% Self-correcting Course*, Lesson 3, 8.
3. Cody, *New Art,* 49, 51.
4. Cody, *New Art*, 32. See also the *Grammar and Punctuation* volume of the *Art of Writing and Speaking the English Language*, 42, for an earlier phrasing.
5. Henry W. Fowler, *A Dictionary of Modern English Usage* (New York: Oxford University Press, 1944), 381, 723.
6. Cody, *100% Self-correcting Course*, Lesson 1, 10. In Lesson 1, he gives the self-test item *I am going to have a piece of cake (ain't—aren't—what) I?* and rejects all of the options in favor of *am I not?*
7. Cody, *100% Self-correcting Course*, Lesson 19, 7. He also allows the possessive for things that may be personified, such as the name of a city and such idi oms as *a day's work* or *for goodness' sake*.
8. Cody, *100% Self-correcting Course*, Lesson 14, 7.
9. Cody, *100% Self-correcting Course*, Lesson 23, 7.
10. Cody, *100% Self-correcting Course*, Lesson 21, 7.
11. Ella Woodyard, *Culture at a Price: A Study of Private Correspondence School Offerings* (New York: American Association for Adult Education, 1940), 22. An example of the sort of changes Cody made is his discussion of generic pronouns. By the 1930s, Cody recognized the need for an occasional *his or her*, though he continued to treat the singular use of the pronoun *they* as an error (*New Art*, 46).
12. Richard Braddock, Richard Lloyd-Jones, and Lowell Schoer wrote that "The teaching of formal grammar has a negligible or, because it usually displaces some instruction and practice in actual composition, even a harmful effect on the improvement of writing": *Research in Written Composition* (Urbana, Ill.: NCTE, 1963), 37–38. See also Stephen D. Krashen, *Writing: Research,*

Theory and Applications (Beverly Hills: Laredo, 1984). The study by Robert J. Connors and Andrea A. Lunsford appears as "Frequency of Formal Errors in Current College Writing, or Ma and Pa Kettle Do Research," *College Composition and Communication* 39(1988): 395–409. Maxine Hairston's "Not All Errors Are Created Equal: Nonacademic Readers in the Professions Respond to Lapses in Usage" was in *College English* 43(1981): 794–806. See also Larry Beason, "Ethos and Error: How Business People React to Errors," *College Composition and Communication* 53(2001): 33–64.

13. Rei R. Noguchi, *Grammar and the Teaching of Writing* (Urbana: NCTE, 1991), 36 and Constance Weaver, *Teaching Grammar in Context* (Portsmouth, N.H.: Boynton/Cook, 1996), 142–47.
14. Cody, *Coaching Children in English* (New York: Good English Publisher), 16–17.
15. Cody, *100% Self-correcting Course*, Lesson 12, 10: "Dies are used to stamp out metal, but dice are cubes for gaming." "Generals in the army have their staffs, but barrels have staves." "We speak of a hundred weight of fish (in bulk), but fifty different species of fishes." The Friday lessons also included some discussion of voice and oral reading, with Cody encouraging students to develop a natural voice which avoids "sing-song" changes in pitch, over-emphasis, or mechanical pronunciation. The last few lessons also contained some exercises calling on students to rewrite sentences.
16. Cody, *100% Self-correcting Course*, Lesson 23, 10.
17. For example, see the glossary to John Franklin Genung's *Outlines of Rhetoric* (Boston: Ginn, 1894), 301–32, or Frank H. Vizetelly's *A Desk-Book of Errors in English* (New York: Funk & Wagnalls, 1906).
18. Cody, *100% Self-correcting Course*, Lesson 14, 10; Lesson 5, 10; Lesson 9, 10; Lesson 11, 10; Lesson 6, 10; and Lesson 2, 10.
19. Cody, *100% Self-correcting Course*, Lesson 11, 10.
20. Cody, *100% Self-correcting Course*, Lesson 15, 10. Cody's views on science follow those of John Franklin Genung, who distinguished the science of critical rhetoric, "the laws and principles of discourse . . . exhibited in an ordered system," from the art of constructive rhetoric, which was "knowledge made efficient by skill": *The Practical Elements of Rhetoric* (Boston, Ginn & Co., 1896), 4.

Chapter Seven

1. In his advertising prospectus, Cody claimed that the literary lessons in his course gave it a competitive advantage over other language instruction: "Sherwin Cody gives something more. He gives his student the finishing touch that makes the man of education." *How You Can Master Good English*, 20.

2. *100% Self-correcting Course*, Lesson 1, 1.
3. Later editions also included Mark Twain, whom Cody called the Charles Dickens of America.
4. Cody, *How to Read and What to Read* (Rochester: Sherwin Cody School of English, 1937), 9. Cody's penchant for efficiency shines through in his discussion of literature as well, and he recommends moderation in reading in order "to let a few great things sink in deeply, yet not in such a way to make them narrow specialists." Cody also suggests reading judiciously, by skimming an author's work and deciding where to invest one's time. It is "far better" he says, "to read a few books or even a few pages carefully, slowly, even painfully, than to slip easily over many." *100% Self-correcting Course*, Lesson 24, 9.
5. Cody, *100% Self-correcting Course*, Lesson 5, 9. Cody also considered Woodrow Wilson "one of the great world writers, in the same class as Lincoln," noting that Wilson was not afraid to use "the kind of language American advertising would like us to use" (Lesson 6, 9).
6. Cody, *100% Self-correcting Course*, Lesson 2, 9.
7. Cody, *How and What to Read*, 15–16.
8. Cody, *How You Can Master Good English*, 21.
9. Cody, *100% Self-correcting Course*, Lesson 2, 9. Literature provided enjoyment, truth and inspiration, but it was also a practical way to make our lives more comprehensible in a changing world, which was necessary if work was to be meaningful. At the same time, literature could provide a broad understanding of the world and of human nature necessary to business success, and in addition, the study of narrative, metaphor, and rhetoric enabled business writers to know their customers and develop "a clear, decisive tone, with a sharp emphasis on the points you want to get across" (Lesson 19, 1). Though he did not use the terms, Cody emphasized the blending of practical and liberal learning, using each to justify the other.
10. See Ralph Waldo Emerson, *The Complete Works of Ralph Waldo Emerson: Society and Solitude,* vol. 7 (New York: Houghton, Mifflin, 1903–04), 189–221, and Noah Porter, *Books and Reading or, What Books Shall I Read and How Shall I Read Them?* (New York: Scribner, 1877).
11. See Joan Shelley Rubin, *The Making of Middlebrow Culture* (Chapel Hill: University of North Carolina Press, 1991), 2–4, for a brief overview. As Rubin notes, there was also a parallel religious tradition, with American religious philosophers like Harvard's Joseph Buckminster developing a view of virtue and salvation through reading and contemplation. Others, like sociologist Thorstein Veblen, viewed the reading habits of the middle class as part of their attempt to emulate the wealthy.
12. Cody, *100% Self-correcting Course*, Lesson 24, 2.
13. Cody, *100% Self-correcting Course*, Lesson 24, 2.

14. The *New York Times Saturday Review of Books and Art* began in 1896 and moved to the Sunday paper shortly afterwards.
15. For Erskine's views, see *The Delight of Great Books* (Indianapolis: Bobbs-Merrill, 1927) and Gerald Graff's *Professing English* (Chicago: University of Chicago Press, 1989). As Rubin notes in *The Making of Middlebrow Culture* (chapters 2–4), projects like the Great Books seminar and the Book-of-the-Month Club generated new public discussions over what sort of books people should be reading and what they ought to be getting out of books. Public critics like Sherman, Erskine, and the Book-of-the-Month Club's lead judge Henry Canby tried to balance the elitism of a literary canon with the goal of broad public participation in culture, and their own attitudes evolved as their perspectives broadened from the academic to the public sphere.
16. He also included Emily Dickinson, Elizabeth Barrett Browning, Edna St. Vincent Millay, Jane Austen, the Brontës, Agnes Repplier, Louisa May Alcott, Harriet Beecher Stowe, George Elliot, Elizabeth C. Gaskell, and Edith Wharton.
17. Cody, *How to Read and What to Read*, 118–122. The 1927 list of recommended reading does not include many of these writers.
18. Christopher Newfield, *Ivy and Industry: Business and the Making of the American University, 1880–1980* (Durham: Duke University Press, 2003), 41.
19. Cody, *How to Read and What to Read*, 7. The terms *highbrow* and *lowbrow* had been adapted from the anthropological practice of estimating intelligence by measuring the size and shape of the cranium. The term *middlebrow*, first used in the 1920s, seems to have come into wide use among critics in the 1930s, in a 1933 essay by Margaret Widdemer in *The Saturday Review of Literature* and later by such critics as Virginia Woolf, Russell Lynes, Clement Greenberg, and Dwight Macdonald. See Rubin's *The Making of Middlebrow Culture*, xii–xiv.

Chapter Eight

1. James D. Norris, *Advertising and the Transformation of American Society, 1865–1920* (New York: Greenwood Press, 1990), 65.
2. Roland Marchand, *Advertising and the American Dream*, 208. Marchand capitalizes his "parables," and I have retained that capitalization here. Elsewhere I refer to them in lowercase as a matter of style.
3. See Benjamin Franklin, *Autobiography and Other Writings*, ed. Russel B. Nye (Boston: Houghton Mifflin, 1958), Eleazar Moody, *The School of Good Manners* (New London, Conn.: Timothy Green, 1715), and Henry Peacham, *The Compleat Gentleman* (London: Constable, 1622). One example of the role of etiquette in education is young George Washington's copying out of

110 rules of conduct as an exercise. The importance of character is shown in the first rule, which was that "Every Action done in Company, ought to be with Some Sign of Respect, to those that are Present." George Washington, *Rules of Civility & Decent Behaviour in Company and Conversation* (Boston: Houghton Mifflin, 1926), 3. Charles Moore's introduction to Washington's rules notes that the etiquette list is contained in one of the two school exercise books preserved in the George Washington Papers at the Library of Congress. For more on etiquette books, see Sarah E. Newton's *Learning to Behave: A Guide to American Conduct Books Before 1900* (Westport, Conn.: Greenwood Press, 1994) and John F. Kasson, *Rudeness and Civility: Manners in Nineteenth-Century Urban America* (New York: Hill & Wang, 1990).

4. Schlesinger, *Learning How to Behave*, 11. Ben Franklin's advice on success, for example, often blended concern for others with self-interest and impression management.
5. Marchand, *Advertising and the American Dream*, 217–18. Even the rich could suffer from athlete's foot, bad breath, or bad grammar, and Marchand describes a democracy of afflictions that linked the rich, poor, and middle-class. Inexpensive remedies were available to those smart enough to buy them. Just as the democracy of goods put status in the reach of anyone, the democracy of afflictions implied a leveling of the inherent advantages of wealth and position. Marchand also discusses two other narrative types: the parables of Civilization Redeemed and of the Captive Child.
6. Erin Smith notes that many text-heavy pulp magazine ads of the 1920s reinforced the audience's notion of themselves as readers. See *Hard-boiled: Working-class Readers and Pulp Magazines* (Philadelphia: Temple University Press, 2000), 65–66.
7. Prudential ads can be found in Charles Goodrum and Helen Dalrymple, *Advertising in America: The First 200 Years* (New York: Harry N. Abrams, 1990), 151, 153.
8. Frank Rowsome, Jr., *They Laughed When I Sat Down: An Informal History of Advertising in Words and Pictures* (New York: Bonanza Books, 1959), 177, 178.
9. The "University of the Night" ad appears in Watkins, *The 100 Greatest Advertisements*, 36. The ad was written by Raymond Rubicam and headlined by George Cecil.
10. "Here's an Extra $50" first appeared in 1919 and is reprinted in Watkins, *The 100 Greatest Advertisements*, 112.
11. "You're a Fine Fellow" appeared in *The World's Work*, Jan. 1932, 5.

Chapter Nine

1. Hugh Hawkins, *Between Harvard and America: The Educational Leadership of Charles W. Eliot* (New York: Oxford University Press, 1972), 292. As Edward

H. Cotton noted, the selections chosen as classics were criticized for complexity and dullness and for omitting nineteenth-century fiction: *The Life of Charles W. Eliot* (Boston: Small, Maynard & Company, 1926), 274. A supplementary Harvard Classics Fiction Shelf was added as well later as well as a set of Junior Classics. By 1926, Collier had sold 14,541,426 volumes (285,126 sets) of the Harvard Classics, along with 1,187,040 volumes of fiction and 1,190,500 of the Junior Classics (Cotton, *Life of Charles W. Eliot*, 276–77). The idea of the Harvard Classics was still an object of derision in 1940 when Mortimer J. Adler published his *How to Read a Book* (New York: Simon and Schuster), in which he argued that the Harvard Classics method "will make you a literary butterfly, not a competent reader" and that the reading plan of the Harvard Classics was "about as intelligible as a college course under the elective system" (131).

2. The actual selection of readings was done by Eliot's editorial assistant, Harvard English professor William Allan Neilson, who later became president of Smith College; see Margaret Farrand Thorp's *Neilson of Smith* (New York: Oxford University Press, 1956).
3. See Adam Kirsch, "The Five-foot Shelf Reconsidered," *Harvard Magazine*, Nov.–Dec. 2001.
4. Hawkins, *Between Harvard and America*, 293.
5. The Harvard Classics ads "No more Latin, No more Greek" appeared in *Youth's Companion,* Nov. 9, 1911, 45, and "If you are a lover of books" in *Current Opinion*, June 1913, 38. "Why treat your mind like a merry-go-round" appeared in the *New York Times Magazine*, November 4, 1923; "What 15 Minutes a Day Has Done to My Husband's Earning Power" was in the *New York Times Book Review*, January 10, 1926, 21; "Why Envy Them Longer?" was in the *Book Review* for Oct. 24, 1941, 17; "It May Never Again Be So Easy to Own the Famous Harvard Classics" was in the *World Almanac and Book of Facts* for 1942, 16A; and "How to Get Rid of an INFERIORITY COMPLEX" appeared in the *World Almanac and Book of Facts* for 1938, 12.
6. From the ad copy for "Do you know her tragic story," written by Bruce Barton and reprinted in Watkins, *The 100 Greatest Advertisements*, 28.
7. Charles W. Eliot, *Fifteen Minutes a Day Reading Guide* (New York: Collier, 1926), 20.
8. Eliot, *Fifteen Minutes*, 5, 7.
9. Sackheim, *My First Sixty Years*, 104–09. Cody had also worked on the idea of developing cheap editions of Shakespeare around 1900, but few seem to have been published. See Daniel, "Sherwin Cody," 6.
10. The Club was acquired by the media conglomerate Bertelsmann in 2000 and merged with other book clubs.

11. Janice Radway, *A Feeling for Books: The Book-of-the-Month Club, Literary Taste, and Middle-Class Desire* (Chapel Hill: University of North Carolina Press, 1997), 160. Radway confirms the role of books as symbols, citing an internal Club finding that people joined not to read any particular book but because they were interested in acquiring an extensive home library (312). She also notes that early mailing lists for the Club included the New York Social Register and a number of university alumni lists, and she suggests marketing targeted "that fraction whose social position was based on its command of cultural and intellectual capital, on a certain acquaintance with the cultural tradition and a measure of specialized knowledge and expertise" (295).
12. Sackheim, *My First Sixty Years*, 107.
13. According to Sackheim, the first Book-of-the-Month Club ad appeared in the *New York Times* of April 25, 1926: *My First Sixty Years*, 117–18.

Chapter Ten

1. One indication of the significance of etiquette is that fact that 146 different adult etiquette books were published between 1918 and 1945. See Arthur M. Schlesinger, Sr., *Learning How to Behave*, 51.
2. By Funk & Wagnalls. The book, after various reprinting and editions, led to a radio show, newspaper column, and in 1946, the Emily Post Institute.
3. Rowsome, *They Laughed When I Sat Down*, 155.
4. Rowsome, *They Laughed When I Sat Down*, 154.
5. *Red Book*, Feb. 1922, 13, cited by Mark Caldwell, *A Short History of Rudeness: Manners, Morals and Misbehaviors in Modern America* (New York: Picador, 1999), 27–28.
6. Lillian Eichler, *The Book of Etiquette*, vol. 1, 2, 3, 5 (Oyster Bay: Nelson Doubleday, 1921).
7. Eichler, *Book of Etiquette,* vol. 2, 135; "Do You Make These Mistakes in English," *New York Times Magazine*, Nov. 11, 1928, 32.
8. Rowsome, *They Laughed When I Sat Down*, 153.
9. John Caples, *Making Ads Pay* (New York: Harper & Brothers, 1957), 41–43, 47–50. His French-at-Sight ad became such an item of popular culture that it was commented on in the press, vaudeville, cartoons, and radio and even parodied in magazines.
10. Robert Lewis Taylor, "Profiles: I was once a 97-pound weakling" *New Yorker,* Jan. 1, 1942, 21–27; see also Elizabeth Toon and Janet Golden "Rethinking Charles Atlas," *Rethinking History* 4(2000), 80–84.
11. On muscular Christianity see, Clifford Putney's *Muscular Christianity: Manhood and Sports in Protestant America, 1880–1920* (Cambridge: Harvard University Press, 2001); for a biography of the colorful Bernarr Macfadden,

see Robert Ernst, *Weakness is a Crime: The Life of Bernarr Macfadden* (Syracuse: Syracuse University Press, 1991).

12. *World Almanac and Encyclopedia* (New York: New York World, 1918), 186–87.
13. "The Insult That Made a Man Out of Mac" is reprinted in Rowsome, *They Laughed When I Sat Down*, 159. "Life's Most Embarrassing Moments" and "She said: 'I'm sorry I can't go out with you tonight'" are on the Atlas website: www.charlesatlas.com/classicads3.htm and www.charlesatlas.com/classicads4.htm [accessed Sept. 7, 2007].
14. Elizabeth Toon and Janet Golden "'Live Clean, Think Clean, and Don't Go to Burlesque Shows': Charles Atlas as Heath Advisor," *Journal of the History of Medicine* 57(2002): 51–58.
15. For many years, the Atlas ads ran in comic books, pulps, tabloids, and muscle magazines, and according to Roman, the average student was 15–25.
16. The observations about George H. W. Bush, David Mamet, and Arun Gandhi are due to Elizabeth Toon and Janet Golden: "Rethinking Charles Atlas," *Rethinking History* 4(2000): 81, 82.
17. "There IS an aristocracy in America! It is an Aristocracy of KNOWLEDGE" appeared in the *New York Times Book Review*, Feb. 1, 1931, 15. "The Famous Pocket University—A Liberal Reading Education," was in the *New York Times Book Review*, Nov. 4, 1923, 32, and "Speak French at Once!" was in the *World Almanac and Book of Facts* for 1939, 7A. "How would you like to spend an hour with Cleopatra?" appeared in *The World's Work* for Sept. 1929.

Chapter Eleven

1. The details of Carnegie's life story rely on the biography by Giles Kemp and Edward Claflin titled *Dale Carnegie: The Man Who Influenced Millions* (New York: St. Martin's Press, 1989) and sociologist Richard M. Huber's *The American Idea of Success* (New York: Pushcart Press, 1987).
2. Dale Carnegie, *How to Stop Worrying and Start Living* (New York: Pocket Books, 1974), 88.
3. Dale Carnegie, *Little Known Facts about Well Known People* (New York: Blue Ribbon Books, 1934).
4. The story of Michael O'Neil is from a Carnegie ad reprinted by Watkins in *The 100 Greatest Advertisements*, 92.
5. Franklin, *Advice to a Young Tradesman,* in *Autobiography and Other Writings,* 167.
6. Conwell did so himself by founding Temple University in Philadelphia. The title of his famous speech warned against sojourns in search of acres of diamonds when riches might be in one's own backyard.
7. Andrew Carnegie, "Wealth," *North American Review,* June 1889, 653–64.

8. The quote is cited in Matthew Josephson, *The Robber Barons* (New York: Harcourt, Brace and Co., 1934), 325, and in Peter Collins and David Horowitz, *The Rockefellers: An American Dynasty* (New York: Holt, Rinehart and Winston, 1976), 47.
9. See Clifford Putney, "Service over Secrecy: How Lodge-Style Fraternalism Yielded Popularity to Men's Service Clubs," *Journal of Popular Culture* 27(1993): 179–90. The champion of the service ethic was undoubtedly B. C. Forbes.
10. Cody, *Business Practice Up to Date: Or, How to Be a Private Secretary, With Commercial Map of the United States* (Chicago: School of English, 1913), 158–59. Cody mentions the "American man of business," but adds that business "is a game in which American women have a part that has never been told and in which more and more girls will take an equal part with boys."
11. H. A. Overstreet, *Influencing Human Behavior* (New York: W. W. Norton, 1925), 9. Overstreet (page 22) cites Cody's *How to Deal with Human Nature in Business*.
12. Warren Susman, "'Personality' and the Making of Twentieth Century Culture," in *Culture as History: The Transformation of American Society in the Twentieth Century* (New York: Pantheon Books, 1984), 279. Huber has also documented the shifting away from character and toward personality in *The American Idea of Success*, and John Ramage, a rhetorician, has noted that in its religious and spiritual manifestations, success rhetoric of the 1950s increasingly became a matter of having religion serve people rather than people serving religion: *Twentieth-Century American Success Rhetoric*, 111–17.
13. William H. Whyte, Jr., *The Organization Man* (New York: Simon and Schuster, 1956), 252–53; C. Wright Mills, *White Collar: The American Middle Class* (New York: Oxford University Press, 1956), 260, 262. Whyte cites Reinhard Bendix's *Work and Authority in Industry: Ideologies of Management in the Course of Industrialization* (New York: Wiley, 1956) as noting the influence of New Thought.
14. Huber, for example, writes that the book was "the symbol that marked the transition" in focus from character to personality: *American Idea of Success*, 226.
15. Carnegie, *How to Win Friends*, xiv.
16. Carnegie, *How to Win Friends*, 33. Carnegie adds that "Every act you have performed since the day you were first born was performed because you wanted something."
17. Carnegie, *How to Win Friends*, xiv; Cody, *How You Can Master Good English*, 5.
18. Cody, *Business Practice Up to Date*, 175. Cody added that "The most cheerful people in the world are the Christian Scientists, who have made a religion out of denying that there is any such thing as pain, suffering, and failure."

19. Carnegie, *How to Stop Worrying and Start Living*, 104. Carnegie's connection to New Thought is emphasized by Ramage in *Twentieth-Century American Success Rhetoric*, 114.
20. In his 1913 book *Public Speaking and Influencing Men in Business*, Carnegie included three appendices—Hubbard's "A Message to Garcia," Conwell's "Acres of Diamonds," and a mind power essay titled "As a Man Thinketh" by James Allen. He noted that these were not directly related to public speaking but thought that they would be of great interest to readers.
21. "Car-Yes-Man," *Newsweek*, Nov. 15, 1937, 31. Modern writers echo this criticism as well. Micki McGee sees Carnegie as describing "a Hobbesian world in which smiles and good cheer were a kind of currency, with every man and woman able to advance themselves by understanding that all others were only out for themselves": *Self-help, Inc.: Makeover Culture in American Life* (New York: Oxford University Press. 2005), 61.
22. Carnegie wrote that "A show of interest, as with every other principle, must be sincere. It must pay off not only for the person showing the interest, but for the person receiving the attention. It is a two-way street—both parties benefit" (*How to Win Friends*, 64). But as Ramage points out, Carnegie conflated sincerity with mutual benefit, and Carnegie's definition of sincerity is not fully convincing because he is unable to provide techniques for sincerity other than appearing sincere: *Twentieth-Century American Success Rhetoric*, 109.
23. See his *How to Stop Worrying and Start Living*.
24. Biographers Kemp and Claflin note that Carnegie would have "felt comfortable" with psychologists of the transactional analysis school, and they emphasize parallels with the approach of Norman Vincent Peale in the 1950s and other "positive thinkers": *Dale Carnegie*, 111, 189–95. The nature of personal success has also changed, moving from the notion of correct behavior and courtesy toward others to self-realization, healthy relationships, and happiness. Religious, business, and personal approaches to success often overlap, blend, and influence one another. Ramage, for example, has noted the blending of morality and efficiency in the work of Stephen Covey and of interpersonal awareness and corporate efficiency in the work of Tom Peters (in *Twentieth-Century American Success Rhetoric*). And in *Self-help, Inc.*, McGee has emphasized the consistent ability of self-help books to recycle and reinvent earlier themes.
25. Huber, *American Idea of Success*, 238.

Chapter Twelve

1. Some students bought supplementary materials, and doubtless many who began the course never completed it. In addition, there were often specials and discounts given.

2. See David Simpson, *The Politics of American English, 1776–1850* (New York: Oxford University Press, 1986) for discussion of Jefferson (32, 243) and Webster (57, 68). See also Harry R. Warfel, *Noah Webster: Schoolmaster to America* (New York: Macmillan, 1936), 127.
3. Kenneth Cmiel, *Democratic Eloquence: The Fight over Popular Speech in Nineteenth-Century America* (New York: William Morrow and Company, 1990), 79. Cmiel also notes that grammar was spread by etiquette books as well.
4. Allan A. Metcalf, *Presidential Voices* (New York: Houghton Mifflin, 2004), 93. Jackson was accused of murder and adultery as well as bad grammar.
5. "Good Manners in Journalism," *New York Times*, April 15, 1868. Slang was a particular concern, with Boston's Oliver Wendell Holmes, Sr., writing that its use "is at once a sign and a cause of mental atrophy": "Mechanism in Thought and Morals," *Pages from an Old Volume of Life* (Boston: Houghton Mifflin, 1891), 275.
6. Mark Twain, "Concerning the American Language," *The Stolen White Elephant* (New York: Charles L. Webster, 1888), 265–67.
7. Webster's modest 1806 dictionary was followed by the two-volume *An American Dictionary of the English Language* in 1828. A new edition was published in 1841, edited by his son-in-law Chauncey Goodrich, a professor of rhetoric at Yale, and in 1864 the Webster editorial group, controlled by George and Charles Merriam, published a revision edited by Noah Porter, with etymologies revised by the German lexicographer C. A. F. Mahn. This first unabridged Webster's dictionary adopted the popular features of Worcester's dictionary, omitted many of Webster's idiosyncrasies, and corrected word histories which had been based on Biblical misunderstandings.
8. "The War of the Dictionaries," *New York Times*, Aug. 7, 1860.
9. Fowler, cited by Dennis Baron, *Grammar and Good Taste* (New Haven: Yale University Press, 1982), 163.
10. See Jacob Riis, *How the Other Half Lives* (New York: Charles Scribner's Sons, 1890) and, for a discussion of dialect literature, William Dean Howells, "New York Low Life in Fiction," *New York World*, July 26, 1896.
11. Marsh, *Lectures on the English Language* (New York: Charles Scribner, 1860), 644. The United States as a whole was still defined linguistically in comparison to England. In 1864 Henry Alford, dean of Canterbury, published *A Plea for the Queen's English*, which argued that the purity of the English language was in danger from the exaggeration and incongruity of American usage. Alford attributed the decline of American speech to the same moral laxity that caused the Civil War. Writer George Washington Moon replied in a work that eventually became titled *The Dean's English*, and the ensuing controversy signaled a trend of usage criticism that endured for the

remainder of the nineteenth century. See Edward Finegan, *Attitudes toward English Usage: The History of a War of Words* (New York: Teachers College Press, 1980), 68–70.

12. Richard Grant White, *Words and Their Uses* (Boston: Houghton Mifflin, 1870), 205, 207, 214, 215. White went so far as to deny the authority of usage and to assume that there was only one correct way of expressing something; see the chapter titled "Jus et Norma Loquendi" ("The law and rule of speech").
13. William Matthews, *Words, Their Use and Abuse* (Chicago: S. C. Griggs, 1876), 335, 91.
14. Cmiel, *Democratic Eloquence*, 133–34. The count of usage manuals in the National Union Catalog is from Cmiel, 264.
15. Henry James, *The Question of Our Speech* (Boston: Houghton Mifflin, 1906), 44. The book was based on a commencement speech given at Bryn Mawr University.
16. Cody, *How You Can Master Good English*, 23. He added that they gain "the self-confidence and self-respect which this ability inspires, and which no one who is uncertain of his English can ever possess."
17. Cody, *How You Can Master Good English*, 18. Cody also drew on the cachet of Shakespeare, reminding readers that the poet never studied rules of grammar and rhetoric.
18. Lawrence Levine, *Highbrow/Lowbrow: The Emergence of Cultural Hierarchy in America* (Cambridge: Harvard University Press, 1988), 211. As Levine notes, there were similar changes going on in the newly expanded library and museum systems, as well. The question naturally arose of whether they ought to encourage or discourage the general public from attending by the hours they kept, the exhibitions and collections they developed, and so forth.
19. Levine, *Highbrow/Lowbrow*, 85–168. Interestingly, he also identifies the decline of formal oratory as one of the causes of this shift in the theatre; see page 76.

Chapter Thirteen

1. William Dwight Whitney, *Language and the Study of Language: Twelve Lectures on the Principles of Linguistic Science* (New York: Charles Scribner, 1867). As the author of a grammar textbook and editor of the *Century Dictionary*, however, Whitney would occasionally condemn popular usage as well.
2. *Better Speech Week* was developed by Claudia E. Crumpton and reported on in "Speech Betterment in Alabama," *English Journal* 6(1917): 96–102. The pledge is cited in Betty Gawthrop's chapter "1911–1929," in Raven I. McDavid, Jr., ed., *An Examination of the Attitudes of the NCTE Toward*

Language: An Analysis of the Development of Ideas on Language Study as Reported in Journal Articles Published by NCTE (Urbana: National Council of Teachers of English, 1965), 9–10.

3. See Fred Newton Scott, "The Standard of American Speech," *English Journal* 6,(1917): 1–11; George Philip Krapp, "The Improvement of English Speech," *English Journal* 7(1918): 87–97; and Sterling Leonard, "Old Purist Junk," *English Journal* 7(1918): 295–302.
4. Gawthrop, "1911–1929," 11; Ella Heaton Pope, "Linguistics as a Required Subject in Colleges and in High School," *English Journal* 8(1919): 28–34.
5. Gawthrop, "1911–1929," 12.
6. George Philip Krapp, *The Knowledge of English* (New York: Holt, 1927), 178.
7. Thomas Lounsbury, "Compulsory Composition in Colleges," *Harper's Monthly,* Nov. 1911, 866–80, cited by Cody in "Scientific Principles in the Teaching of Composition," *English Journal* 1(1912): 161.
8. Cody, *New Art*, 4–5; Cody was referring to Leonard's book *Current English Usage* (Chicago: The Inland Press, 1932). I have not found references to linguists Edward Sapir and Leonard Bloomfield in Cody's work, though they were publishing at the same time.
9. Cody, *Commercial Tests*, 51. He added that speech "should not be extreme to the point of being pedantic or affected."
10. Cody, *New Art*, 3.
11. Cody, "Scientific Principles," 162. He also called attention to class size as affecting the health of teachers and driving the best ones out of the field, 166–67.
12. C. Michael Lightner, "1930–1945," in *An Examination of the Attitudes of the NCTE Toward Language,* 23. See also Wilbur W. Hatfield, *An Experience Curriculum in English* (Champaign, Ill.: National Council of Teachers of English, 1935). Historically there have been two main reasons given for grammar teaching in the schools: its supposed usefulness in helping students to master standard forms of English and its supposed usefulness in improving writing.
13. See Richard Braddock, Richard Lloyd-Jones, and Lowell Schoer, *Research in Written Composition* (Urbana, Ill.: National Council of Teachers of English, 1963), 37–38.
14. Leonard, "Old Purist Junk," 295–96. Leonard does not mention Cody by name, but in an earlier essay, "In Praise of Prevision," *English Journal* 4(1915): 500–07, Leonard had noted that Cody's suggestion that students write essays twice was "a valid and useful device" (501).
15. Robert A. Hall, Jr., *Linguistics and Your Language* (New York: Anchor Books, 1960; rev. ed. of *Leave Your Language Alone!*, Linguistica, 1950), 9. The chapter

begins this way: "How many of these frequent errors in English do YOU make? Do YOU say KEW-pon for KOO-pon, ad-ver-TISE-ment for ad-VER-tise-ment, or AD-ult for ad-ULT? Almost everybody makes these blunders in English: *between you and I, it's me, those kind of books*. Even the greatest writers sin against the laws of grammar. We have all seen advertisements in newspapers and magazines, with messages like those just quoted, implying to the reader 'shame on you if you are one of those who sin!'—and of course offering to teach him better."

16. Hall, *Linguistics and Your Language*, 29.

17. Cody, *Commercial Tests*, 13.

18. Hugh Blair, *Lectures on Rhetoric and Belles Lettres*, ed. Linda Ferreira-Buckley and S. Michael Halloran (Carbondale: Southern Illinois University Press, 2005). See also Robert J. Connors, *Composition-Rhetoric: Backgrounds, Theory, and Pedagogy* (Pittsburgh: University of Pittsburgh Press, 1997), 74–75, and James A. Berlin, *Writing Instruction in Nineteenth-Century American Colleges* (Carbondale: Southern Illinois University Press, 1984), 25–28. Two other popular rhetoric texts were George Campbell's *Philosophy of Rhetoric* (1776) and Richard Whately's *Elements of Rhetoric* (1828), which were sometimes used together with Blair's.

19. Linda Ferreira-Buckley and S. Michael Halloran, Introduction to Blair, *Lectures*, xxxvi, xxxviii.

20. Blair, *Lectures*, 7.

21. Connors, *Composition-Rhetoric*, 126.

22. Charles W. Eliot, "Inaugural Address as President of Harvard College," *Educational Reform: Essays and Addresses* (New York: The Century, 1898), 121, cited by Albert R. Kitzhaber, *Rhetoric in American Colleges, 1850–1900* (Dallas: Southern Methodist University Press, 1990), 33.

23. Kitzhaber, *Rhetoric in American Colleges*, 35.

24. College composition texts adapted to this model and reinforced the idea of grammar as the avoidance of error rather than as an element of style and variation. See Kitzhaber, *Rhetoric in American Colleges*, 203–04, and Connors, *Composition-Rhetoric*, 94–95.

25. Cody, "Scientific Principles," 164.

26. Cody, "Scientific Principles," 165.

27. Cody, "Scientific Principles," 165–66.

28. Genung, *Practical Elements of Rhetoric* (Boston: Ginn, 1896), 1.

29. Berlin, *Writing Instruction*, 64–65, discusses Genung's approach to invention. Genung, along with Harvard's Adams Sherman Hill and Barrett Wendell, helped to set the theoretical stage for modern composition for many years. See Kitzhaber, *Rhetoric*, 63–65, for a brief note on Genung as a teacher and scholar.

30. Genung, *Outlines of Rhetoric* (Boston: Ginn, 1894), iv. The technique of numbering the rules was intended to provide an efficient way for teachers to refer students to the explanatory principles underlying their errors, and was later used with great effect by John Hodges in the *Harbrace Handbook* series.
31. Genung, *Practical Elements*, vii.
32. "Education by Mail," *New York Observer and Chronicle*, Aug. 30, 1906.

Chapter Fourteen

1. Frederick Jackson Turner, "The Extension Work of the University of Wisconsin," in *Handbook of University Extension*, ed. George F. James and Edmund J. James (Philadelphia: American Society for the Extension of University Teaching, 1893), 315, cited by Barbara L. Watkins in "A Quite Radical Idea: The Invention and Elaboration of Collegiate Correspondence Study," in *The Foundations of American Distance Education: A Century of Collegiate Correspondence Study*, ed. Barbara L. Watkins and Stephen J. Wright (Dubuque: Kendall-Hunt, 1991), 11.
2. From an ad in the *New York Times Book Review*, Feb. 26, 1927.
3. Sylvia N. Rose, "Collegiate-based Noncredit Courses," in *The Foundations of American Distance Education: A Century of Collegiate Correspondence Study*, ed. Barbara L. Watkins and Stephen J. Wright (Dubuque: Kendall-Hunt, 1991), 80.
4. Thorstein Veblen, *The Higher Learning In America: A Memorandum on the Conduct of Universities by Business Men* (Stanford: Academic Reprints, 1954), 191–92. He writes that "a variety of 'university extension' bureaux have been installed, to comfort and edify the unlearned with lyceum lectures, to dispense education by mail-order, and to maintain some putative contacts with amateur scholars and dilettanti beyond the pale."
5. Abraham Flexner, *Universities: American, English, German* (New York: Oxford University Press, 1968 reprint of the 1930 original), 55. He begins the quote conceding that "Doubtless, now and then, an earnest student may safely dispense with continuous, full-time schooling." See also pages 134–47.
6. *The ICS System of Instruction by Mail and the Results Achieved* (Scranton: ICS, 1905), xv–xix, iii–vi.
7. John Odell, *The International Correspondence Schools As a National Asset* (Scranton: ICS, 1911), 3, 7.
8. Today ICS operates as Penn Foster Career College, offering about 80 courses of study by distance learning.
9. Noffsinger, *Correspondence Schools, Lyceums, Chautauquas* (New York: Macmillan, 1926), 15–16. Noffsinger estimated the number of students being instructed by correspondence schools in 1924 as somewhere between 1,750,000 and

2,000,000. He also estimated that 80% of private schools were controlled by single individuals. In 1938, Ella Woodyard estimated the correspondence school industry as having $30,000,000 in annual revenues and 500,000 enrollees.

10. Noffsinger, *Correspondence Schools*, 33–34.
11. Noffsinger, *Correspondence Schools*, 42.
12. Ella Woodyard, *Culture at a Price: A Study of Private Correspondence School Offerings* (New York: American Association for Adult Education, 1940), 22. She also found fault with Cody's grammar in some instances. An earlier review in 1920 described Cody's course as a model self-instruction system, writing that "Each lesson sets up certain objectives which . . . are put before the student in an interesting way and are arranged so that the student may see for himself whether or not he has made progress." Ernest Horn, "A Suggestive Plan of Individual Instruction in English," *The School Review*, Feb. 1920, 153–54.
13. Woodyard, *Culture at a Price*, 117.
14. Woodyard, *Culture at a Price*, 107–08.

Chapter Fifteen

1. The Civic Theatre of Dobbs Ferry was opened "at the suggestion of Sherwin Cody, well-known educator and a resident of Dobbs Ferry," according to Albert McCleery and Carl Glick, *Curtains Going Up* (New York: Pitman, 1939), 38.
2. See "Pays to Test Your Stenographers," *Forbes,* May 29, 1920, 137–38; "Enlarging the Scope of Mental Measurement," *Journal of Philosophy, Psychology and Scientific Methods*, 17(1920): 572–79; and "How to Spot Defects in Business Brains," *People's Favorite Magazine,* Nov. 1920, 26–31.
3. See "Books in Brief," *The Nation,* Oct. 22, 1924, 450, for a short, negative review.
4. "'House That Grows' Designed for Westchester Site," *New York Times*, March 18, 1934; "Architect Builds His Residence of Native Stone," *New York Times*, May 30, 1937; *Who's Who in America*, vol. 26 (Chicago: A. N. Marquis, 1950), 517. Cody's interest in design and real estate can be traced back to his college years and to his pamphlet on "How to Build a Cheap House." He also wrote an approving architectural review of a Bahai center in Chicago: "An Exotic Temple for a Chicago Suburb," *New York Times Book Review and Magazine*, Aug. 1, 1920, 53.
5. The *New Art* was first issued as a series in 1933 and then as a single volume in 1938.
6. Cody, *100% Self-correcting Course in English Language*, 1936, Lesson 1, 11. The synonyms were *exciting (thrilling), bald (glabrous), calm (allay), weakening*

(enervating), stiffly formal (stilted), abusive (scurrilous), decisive (peremptory), very bright (refulgent), linguist (polyglot), and *withdrew (retracted).*

7. Cody, *100% Self-correcting Course*, 1936, Lesson 4, 11; Lesson 6, 11.
8. Cody, *100% Self-correcting Course*, 1936, Lesson 1, 1.
9. Cody, *100% Self-correcting Course*, 1936, Lesson 6, 11; Lesson 8, 1.
10. Cody, *100% Self-correcting Course*, 1936, Lessons 8, 10, 14, 16, 18, all p 1. Other lessons dealt with making new acquaintances, with embarrassing moments, and with the relation between good talking and acting.
11. Cody, *100% Self-correcting Course*, 1936, Lesson 6, 11.
12. Cody, *100% Self-correcting Course*, 1936, Lesson 18, 11, Lesson 3, 1.
13. The remainder of the book was made up of *English in a Nutshell for Children* and sample tests of the Good English Institute.
14. Cody, *Coaching Children in English*, 13–16.
15. Cody, *Coaching Children*, 22, 27, 28. The link between classroom instruction and the self-correcting method can be found as early as Cody's 1912 "Scientific Principles in the Teaching of Composition."
16. The best example is his 1919 book *Commercial Tests and How to Use Them.*
17. Cody, *Coaching Children*, 12.
18. Cody, *Coaching Children*, 11.
19. Rita Kramer, *Maria Montessori* (New York: G.P. Putnam's Sons, 1976), 217.
20. Cody, *Coaching Children*, 27.
21. Cody, *Coaching Children*, 17.
22. The teaching material geared to this method was presented in pages 107–74 of *Coaching Children*, as the "English in a Nutshell for Children" workbook, a set of exercises in grammar, spelling, punctuation, and correspondence, together with explanatory material for parents to use with students.
23. C. K. Ogden, *Basic English and Grammatical Reform* (Cambridge: The Orthological Institute, 1937), 2. Basic was an acronym for "British American Scientific International Commercial" English; it captured the attention of Winston Churchill, who became a staunch proponent in the 1940s.
24. Cody's letters are in the C. K. Ogden collection at McMaster University; Ogden's replies are not preserved.
25. From the Cody letters in the C. K. Ogden collection.
26. "Letters Found in the Drama Mailbag," *New York Times*, April 13, 1952.
27. According to a letter in the Knopf archive at the Harry Ransom Humanities Research Center at the University of Texas.
28. Daniel, "Sherwin Cody," 6.
29. Information on Morrill Cody can be found in Bill Cody's "Author-Diplomat Morrill Cody: He Was There As History Pages Turned," *Lost*

Generation Journal, Winter 1981, 2–5 and Tom Wood's "Cody Best Known Among Literati," *Lost Generation Journal,* Winter 1981, 6. Like many people, Sherwin Cody seems to have been a more affable grandparent than parent, and he had a particularly strong relationship with his granddaughter Judith.

30. Carter Daniel, personal communication. Daniel interviewed Morrill in the 1980s, and I am grateful to him for sharing his recollections.
31. The context was a book notice of new editions of several of his books on letter writing. The reviewer commented that "The indefatigable Sherwin Cody has revised his textbooks" and that "his little manuals have rendered wide service to those who have grown rusty in their English, as well as to those who have awakened too late to the fact that writing is not a superfluous accomplishment but a practical necessity," *The Nation*, Sept. 7, 1918, 272.
32. Peter Bart, "Advertising Slogan is Disappearing After Forty Years," *New York Times*, Feb. 14, 1962.
33. Dorothy Carnegie passed away in 1998. Charles Atlas's body-building course also survives today. Atlas lived longer than Cody and Carnegie, until 1972, and his long-time business partner Charles Roman helped to guide the course through the last half of the twentieth century. As the bodybuilding culture grew as a niche, Atlas's advertising shifted from the general market to the fitness and health magazines and today is even attracting senior citizens for whom Charles Atlas is a familiar name from their youth.
34. Schwab retired in 1962 and moved to Torremolinos, Spain. In 1972 the agency he and Beatty built was acquired by Marsteller Inc., which then was bought by Young and Rubicam. Schwab died in 1980.
35. "Do People Laugh at You for Reading Comic Books?" *Mad,* June 1954, 17; *Mad* satirized the intellectual success culture more generally in pieces like "How to Be Smart" (*Mad,* April 1956, 9–15).
36. The critique appeared in "The Creative Man's Corner: How Do Youse Feel About It?" *Advertising Age*, April 14, 1958, 84, and Kemp's letter in *Advertising Age*, May 5, 1958, 160. Given Cody's seriousness, it may be that the ad appeared after his 1957 stroke. The Creative Man's Corner piece also elicited a reply by Cody's cousin Aldus Cody, who countered that "the people who say 'can't hardly' and 'youse' are not insulted by this advertising": *Advertising Age*, May 5, 1958, 160.
37. Peter Bart, "Advertising Slogan is Disappearing After Forty Years," *New York Times*, Feb. 14, 1962.
38. Barzun found particular fault with linguists and English educators; see my book *Bad Language: Are Some Words Better than Others?* (New York: Oxford University Press, 2005), 55–58.
39. The distinction between formal and colloquial English was not disappearing, it was just becoming more widely visible through the broadcast

media and more hotly discussed through public debates about the National Council of Teachers of English report on *The English Language Arts* (New York: Appleton-Century-Croft, 1952). The heat continued into the 1960s with the commentary surrounding the publication of Webster's *Third New International Dictionary*, which was described as "a kind of Kinsey Report in linguistics"; see Herbert C. Morton's *The Story of* Webster's Third: *Philip Gove's Controversial Dictionary and Its Critics*, 309, n. 23, quoting a review in the *Detroit News* (Cambridge: Cambridge University Press, 1994).

40. Theodore Peterson, *Magazines in the Twentieth Century* (Urbana: University of Illinois, 1964), 309, for discussion of the pulps, and Benjamin Compaine, *The Newspaper Industry in the 1980s* (White Plains, N.Y.: Knowledge Industry Publications, 1980), 28, for newspaper circulation. According to Compaine, Sunday newspaper circulation grew from about 17 million in 1920 to about 46 million in 1950, and then grew just modestly for the next 20 years to 49 million in 1970.
41. William D. Smith, "Study by Mail is Gaining Favor," *New York Times*, July 1, 1962. The *Times* also reported correspondence school owners' optimistic forecasts of continued profitability based on population growth, automation, the need to retrain unskilled workers, and other factors.

Chapter Sixteen

1. By providing self-study materials for potential test-takers, he also helped to pave the way for the business of test preparation, taken up by contemporary businesses like Kaplan Test Prep and The Princeton Review, among others.
2. In addition, the stoking of grammatical anxiety through books of verbal criticism remains a thriving market niche today.

Answers to Exercises

Answers to "Subordinate Clauses" punctuation exercise (page 56)

This Lesson 6 exercise asked readers to "Decide which clauses in the following are to be set off by commas and which not, inserting also periods and capital letters." Readers were also instructed to mark simple subjects, predicates, subordinate conjunctions, and relative pronouns. In the key, subjects are underlined, predicates are italicized, and subordinating conjunctions and relative pronouns are bolded.

> Yesterday <u>we</u> *went* for a picnic to the woods **which** <u>we</u> *visited* last summer. Even **before** the <u>sun</u> *was* up <u>Harold and Ellen</u> *were* out of bed and getting dressed. **As** <u>I</u> *had packed* our lunch basket the night before, <u>we</u> *had* only to dress and get our breakfast. <u>I</u> *told* mother **that** <u>I</u> *would* not *let* the boys go in swimming, and <u>Ellen</u> *promised* to see **that** the <u>girls</u> *did* not *take* off their shoes. <u>Mother</u> *was* afraid **that** <u>snakes</u> *might bite* their feet.

Answers to Lesson 1 Grammar Self-Test (page 59)

1. Every one of those men (has his—~~have their~~) pickax. Each point (is—~~are~~) as clear as a star. The woman or the tiger (~~come~~—comes) out. Montgomery Ward & Co. (have—~~has~~) settled the strike. The Montgomery Ward Company (~~have~~—has) settled the strike.
2. The ship (sank—sunk). [sank or sunk is accepted] The bird has (~~broke~~—broken) its wing.
3. He has (laid—~~lain~~) it down. When he came in he (~~set~~—sat) down. I saw that the book (lay—~~laid~~) on the table. At eight o'clock I (~~laid~~—lay) down. At eight o'clock I (~~set~~—sat) down.
4. The doctor said that fever (produces—~~produced~~) thirst. It had happened before I (saw—~~had seen~~) him. From what I saw of him he appeared (to be—~~to have been~~) a man of letters.
5. I wish Anna (~~was~~—were) here. If Anna (~~was~~—were) here, she would nurse him. If Anna (was—~~were~~) there, she was the life of the company.
6. ~~While sitting on my doorstep, a beautiful butterfly caught my eye~~—While sitting on my doorstep, I caught sight of a beautiful butterfly. By doing so you will clear up the matter—~~By doing so the matter will be cleared up. On weighing the sugar a shortage was found~~—On weighing the sugar he found a shortage.
7. I saw (him—~~his~~) doing it. I approve (~~him~~—his) doing it. What do you think of (~~me~~—my) going to town?
8. I was frightened at ~~that examination's length~~—the length of that examination. For (goodness'—~~goodness's~~—~~goodness~~) sake. He spoke of ~~the land's fertility~~—the fertility of the land.
9. I do not like (~~those~~—that) sort of people. I belong to (that—~~those~~) kind myself.
10. He feels (bad—~~badly~~) about it. It looks (good—~~well~~) to me. The general stood (firm—~~firmly~~).

Grammar school graduates average 13 mistakes

High school graduates average 8 mistakes

Experienced stenographers average 5 mistakes

Answers to "What are Your Mistakes in Grammar?" (pages 67–68)

From Lesson 8—Grammar

1. The Company (has—~~have~~) issued its financial statement.
2. Our factory (~~have~~—has) established new rules for employees.
3. The United States Army in France (~~have~~—has) fought well.
4. An army of laboring men (~~was~~—were) pouring over the bridge.
5. A few of the men (~~was~~—were) running.
6. A number of the men (~~was~~—were) running.
7. The number of men on the list (~~were~~—was) fifty.
8. A fixed number of men (is—~~are~~) drawn each year.
9. None of the men of our day (speaks—~~speak~~) so clearly as Wilson.
10. None of the Fifth Regiment (were—~~was~~) wounded.
11. The Jones Brothers Tea Company (has—~~have~~) joined the society.
12. Jones Brothers (~~has~~—have) joined the society.
13. Tait & Co. (have—~~has~~) joined the society.
14. Lloyd George's Cabinet (~~has~~—has) decided to resign.
15. Mamie Brown, together with six other girls and five boys, (~~have~~—has) appeared for examination.
16. Each of the sixteen companies of infantry and three companies of artillery (is—~~are~~) now on parade.
17. Several of the sixteen companies of infantry and three companies of artillery (~~is~~—are) on parade.
18. Every one of the forty seventh-grade boys and the A division of girls (was—~~were~~) promoted.
19. The President's staff, including Major-General Wood, Colonel Lansing, and Major Downing, (~~are~~—is) leading the procession.
20. The first essential in choosing your studies (is—~~are~~) definite aims.

21. Captain Jones, as well as the sailors, (has—~~have~~) been wounded.
22. None of these fifty men (are—~~is~~) eligible.
23. Our class of ninety-five (has—~~have~~) just graduated.
24. The congregation of the Episcopal church (~~are~~—is) voting for a pastor.
25. The United States (~~are~~—is) demanding reciprocity.

Answers to "Which is it?" (page 72)

The weather affects his nerve. The medicine effects (produces) a cure. (Lesson 1)

His impudence aggravates (adds to) the offense but do not say "He aggravates (irritates) me." (Lesson 1)

An historical (accent not on the first syllable) or a historical. A hero, a history (accent on syllable containing h). (Lesson 1, with note)

He lives at Libertyville (a small city). He lives in Chicago (a large city) or in Pennsylvania (a state). (Lesson 2)

He is apt in his lessons, but not apt to hear at any time that he is promoted. Say, "likely to hear." (Lesson 2)

A performance is continuous when it has no break, but it may rain continually even though it stops now and then. (Lesson 4)

Only things that inspire awe should be called awful. It was an awful thunderstorm but surely not an awfully sweet cake. (Lesson 3)

She sits beside the bed (by the side of) but there is no one there besides (aside from) her. (Lesson 3)

We bring apples to this place. We carry the apples away to that place. We fetch the apples by going after them and bringing them. (Lesson 3)

The pie was divided *between* the two of them but *among* the three or more of them. (Lesson 3)

We die of a disease not from it or with it. (Lesson 5)

There are divers (various) opinions in regards to war, but the opinions of the Germans and of the allies are diverse (opposed to each other). (Lesson 5)

When two are concerned we speak of *each other,* when several *one another.* (Lesson 5)

It is best to use *farther* for distances, and *further* in a figurative sense for anything additional, as, "We will go no further. Have you anything further to say." (Lesson 6)

They advanced forward or forwards many miles (you may decide for yourself which sounds better). (Lesson 7)

The English call a laborer a "man" and an aristocrat who is just as boorish a "gentleman"; but Americans prefer to reserve the word "gentleman" for the man who has natural instincts of high breeding. (Lesson 7)

Americans are said to *guess* when they mean *think,* but "I guess it is true" seems to be a pretty well accepted idiom. (Lesson 7)

Hardly implies the negative, so "I can't hardly make it out" is tautological for "I can hardly make it out." (Lesson 7)

Got is preferred to *gotten* as the past participle, but even so we should not say "We have got a thing" when we mean simply "We have it." (Lesson 7)

It is a mere affectation to speak of a sales *lady* when sales*woman* is the simple and democratic word. (Lesson 8)

"Lit" is an obsolete form of *lighted.* (Lesson 9)

Ladies in society go to "luncheon" while common folk in a hurry eat "lunch." (Lesson 9)

Née, meaning *born,* is feminine, while *né* with but one *e* is masculine. (Lesson 10)

"I had only two dollars in my pocket" is correct while "I only had" would be wrong, since it makes *only* limit the act of having instead of *two.*" (Lesson 11)

We should say "ten pair of shoes" but "several pairs"—*pair* for the plural when preceded by a number, *pairs* when preceded by other words. (Lesson 11)

"Gents" wear "pants" while "gentlemen" wear "trousers." (Lesson 11)

We *permit* in a formal way, but *allow* by tacit consent. (Lesson 11)

... when we say "I met a party in the street who told me he had just enlisted in the army"; we use *party* when *person* would correctly convey the meaning, and it is contrary to the

(continued)

principles of language to admit a new word without some added meaning. (Lesson 11)

Children are reared not *raised,* though we may *raise* chickens. (Lesson 12)

Americans also have a bad habit of calling every proposal a "proposition." A *proposal* is something to do, while a *proposition* is something to be discussed. (Lesson 13)

That which is usable, useful, or valuable in practice is *practical,* but that which is workable is said to be *practicable* (capable of being practiced). (Lesson 13)

In the United States, young people attending schools are called *pupils* through the elementary and high school and *students* when they get to college, on the theory that they are independently interested in studying things out for themselves instead of merely being taught. (Lesson 15)

Things *seem* to the inner mind, but *appear* to the outer senses. (Lesson 15)

Standpoint and *point of view* are interchangeable, according to the requirements of euphony. (Lesson 16)

We choose *toward* or *towards* purely according to the sound and the same is true of *afterward* and *afterwards, onward* and *onwards, forward, backward, upward,* etc. (Lesson 17)

"We all like to joyfully recall the days of youth" is an unnecessary splitting of the infinitive, for "we all like joyfully to recall" sounds just as natural. There are cases, however, where splitting the infinitive seems necessary in expressing our meaning, usually because of some special emphasis we require. (Lesson 17)

Unbeknownst is merely a vulgar form of *unbeknown.* (Lesson 17)

Use *entire* in describing objects made up of several units, as "the entire audience," "the entire membership." And *whole of* with such a solid unit as an apple—"the *whole of* an apple" (Lesson 18).

Sherwin Cody Timeline

1868	Born, Nov. 30, in Cody's Mills, Michigan, the oldest child of Aldus and Eliza Cody.
1879	Aldus Cody dies of tuberculosis on Jan. 12.
1880	Eliza Cody dies in July. Orphaned, Sherwin moves in with relatives in Canterbury, New Hampshire.
1889	Sherwin Cody graduates from Amherst College.
1891	Thomas Foster begins The International Correspondence School.
1893	Cody moves to New York to pursue a literary career; publishes *Life's Philosophy*, a book of poems.
1894	Publishes *How to Write Fiction*, and travels to London to pursue a literary career.
1896	Publishes *In the Heart of the Hills*; marries Marian Teresa Hurley (Sept. 5) and moves to Chicago, where he works at the *Chicago Record* and then the *Tribune*.
1897	Founds the Old Greek Press.
1901	Marian and Sherwin have a son, Edward Morrill Cody.
1903	Cody publishes the four-volume *The Art of Writing and Speaking the English Language*.
1906	Launches a humor magazine, *The Touchstone*.

1907 Publishes the initial Nutshell Library.

1909 Charles Eliot first publishes The Harvard Classics.

1911 Cody travels to Europe for a year's vacation with Marian and Morrill.

1914 Works with National Cash Register Co., Burroughs Adding Machine Co., National Cloak & Suit Co., and Filene's on employee testing.

1916 Founds the National Associated Schools of Scientific Business.

1917 Works with William Wirt in the Gary, Indiana, school system on testing and assessment.

1918 Approaches the Ruthrauff & Ryan agency, meets Maxwell Sackheim, and launches *The Sherwin Cody 100% Self-correcting Course in English Language.*

1919 Publishes *Commercial Tests and How to Use Them*, drawing on his Gary work.

1923 Publishes *Sherwin Cody's Business Ability Development Course.*

1926 Maxwell Sackheim and Harry Scherman launch The Book-of-the-Month Club.

1928 Cody purchases a home site in Dobbs Ferry, New York, which later becomes the Hilltop Park community.

1933 Publishes *The New Art of Writing and Speaking the English Language.*

1936 Dale Carnegie first publishes *How to Win Friends and Influence People.*

Cody issues a revision of the *100% Self-correcting Course.*

1943 Marian Cody dies of cancer on Feb. 8. Cody enters a correspondence with C. K. Ogden about a new project to teach English by pictures.

1944 Publishes *Coaching Children in English.*

1953 Closes the Rochester office. The U.S. School of Music in Port Washington, New York, takes over the management of the course until Cody's death.

1957 Cody has a stroke and moves in with caretaker Nellie Brink in Brooklyn, New York.

1959 Dies on April 6, in Brooklyn, at the age of 90. The final *New York Times* "Do You Make These Mistakes in English?" ad runs on Dec. 27.

Works by Sherwin Cody

1893

Life's Philosophy. Privately printed book of poems.

1894

How to Write Fiction, Especially the Art of Short Story Writing. New York: The Riverside Literary Bureau, C. T. Dillingham & Co.
"Artist-authors," *Outlook* 49(May 26), 910–11.

1895

How to Write Fiction, Especially the Art of Short Story Writing: A Practical Study of Technique. London: Bellairs, 1895 [reprint of 1894].

1896

In the Heart of the Hills. London: J. M. Dent.

1897

Story Composition. Chicago: A. Flanagan.

1899

The Story of William Cullen Bryant for Young Readers. New York & Chicago: Werner School Book Company. [The Young Readers books were part of the Baldwin's biographical booklets series.]

The Story of Washington Irving for Young Readers. New York & Chicago: Werner School Book Company.
The Story of Edgar Allan Poe for Young Readers. New York & Chicago: Werner School Book Company.
The Story of John Greenleaf Whittier for Young Readers. New York & Chicago: Werner School Book Company.
Four American Poets; William Cullen Bryant, Henry Wadsworth Longfellow, John Greenleaf Whittier, Oliver Wendell Holmes; A Book for Young Americans: New York & Chicago: Werner School Book Company [reprinted in 1977 by Folcroft Library Editions].
Four Famous American Writers: Washington Irving, Edgar Allan Poe, James Russell Lowell, Bayard Taylor; A Book for Young Americans: New York & Chicago: Werner School Book Company.

1902

How to Build a Cheap House. [n.p.]
Selections from the World's Greatest Short Stories; Illustrative of the History of Short Story Writing; with Critical and Historical Comments by Sherwin Cody. Chicago: A.C. McClurg & Company [published also as *A Selection from the World's Greatest Short Stories* and *World's Greatest Short Stories*].

1903

A Selection from the Best English Essays Illustrative of the History of English Prose Style; Chosen and Arranged with Historical & Critical Introductions by Sherwin Cody. Chicago: A.C. McClurg & Company.
"Poe's Contributions to American Literary history," *The Dial* (Sept. 16), 161–62.
The Best Tales of Edgar Allan Poe, Edited with an Introduction by Sherwin Cody. Chicago: A.C. McClurg & Company.
The Best Poems and Essays of Edgar Allan Poe Edited with a New Biographical and Critical Study of the Author, by Sherwin Cody. Chicago: A.C. McClurg & Company.
The Art of Writing & Speaking the English Language. Chicago: The Old Greek Press [also revised and published in 1903 by Funk & Wagnalls; see note on page 206].
Word-Study. Chicago: The Old Greek Press.

1904

A Selection from the World's Great Orations Illustrative of the History of Oratory and the Art of Public Speaking, Chosen and Edited with a Series of Introductions by Sherwin Cody. Chicago: A. C. McClurg & Company.
Good English Form Book in Business Letter Writing. Chicago: School of English.

1905

A Selection from the Great English Poets, with an Essay On the Reading of Poetry; Chosen and Arranged, with a Series of Introductions, by Sherwin Cody. Chicago: A.C. McClurg & Company.
How to Read and What to Read. Chicago & New York: The Old Greek Press.
Exercises in Word-Study to Accompany Sherwin Cody's Word-Study. Chicago: School of English.

1906

Success in Letter Writing: Business and Social. Chicago: A.C. McClurg [New rev. ed. Rochester, N.Y.: Sherwin Cody School of English, 1921].
The Cody System. Chicago [privately printed cards].

1907

Word-Study and Business Speller, for High Schools and Business Colleges. Chicago: School of English.
"How to Get a Step Higher in the Business World," *Agricultural Advertising* 17(Sept.), 234–235.
An Evening with Shakespeare. Chicago: School of English.
An Evening with Lamb. Chicago: School of English.
An Evening with Dickens. Chicago: School of English.
An Evening with Thackeray. Chicago: School of English.
An Evening with Burns. Chicago: School of English.
An Evening with Lincoln. Chicago: School of English.
An Evening with Irving. Chicago: School of English.
An Evening with Tennyson. Chicago: School of English.
An Evening with Longfellow. Chicago: School of English.
An Evening with Scott. Chicago: School of English.

1908

How to Do Business by Letter, and Training Course in Business English Composition. The Old Greek Press.

1909

"Poe as Critic," *Putnam's Magazine* vol. 5 (Jan.), 438–40.

1911

How to Do Business by Letter, and Advertising; A Practical and Scientific Method of Handling Customers by Written Salesmanship. London, Constable and

Company, Ltd., [also published in an Advertising and Salesmanship edition in 1912].

1912

Literary Composition; A Practicable Method of Learning to Write Effectively. Chicago: School of English.
Problems and Principles of Correct English, Grammar, Punctuation, Rhetorical Criticism. Chicago: School of English [a supplement to "Exercises in business letter writing"].
Exercises on How to Do Business. Chicago: School of English.
"Scientific Principles in the Teaching of Composition," *English Journal* 1, 161–72.

1913

How to Be a Private Secretary; Or, Business Practice Up to Date, with Commercial Map of the United States. Chicago: School of English.

1914

"The Ideal Course in English for Vocational Students," *English Journal* 3.5, 263–81, continued in 3.6, 371–80.
English for Business Uses and Commercial Correspondence. Chicago: School of English.
The Voters Hand Book: Compiled Especially for the Use of American Women. Farkas Co.

1915

How to Deal with Human Nature in Business; A Practical Book On Doing Business by Correspondence, Advertising, and Salesmanship. New York & London: Funk & Wagnalls Company, also Chicago: School of English.

1916

"Tests to Use When You Hire," *System* (Aug.), 122–30.

1917

"A Scientific Method of Employing Office Help," *Proceedings of the Second Pan American Scientific Congress* (ed. by Glen Levin Swiggett). Washington: Government Printing Office, Section IV, Part 2, Vol. V, 113–18.
Brief Fundamentals. Chicago: School of English [rev. eds. 1936 and 1949].

1918

The Sherwin Cody 100% Self-Correcting Course in English Language. Rochester, N.Y.: The Sherwin Cody School of English [revised 1936].

How You Can Master Good English—in Just 15 Minutes a Day. [Rochester, N.Y.: The Sherwin Cody School of English [earlier version of the advertising booklet *How to Speak and Write Masterly English*].

Course in the New Business Efficiency, Or, How to Make Money in Business (Mind Power in Business). New York: B.C. Forbes.

1919

Commercial Tests and How to Use Them. Yonkers-on-Hudson, N.Y.: World Book Company.

1920

Standard Test English. New York: Association Press.

Teachers' Manual to Accompany Standard Test English. New York: Association Press.

"Enlarging the Scope of Mental Measurement," *Journal of Philosophy, Psychology and Scientific Methods* 17.21 (Oct. 7), 572–79.

"Pays to Test Your Stenographers," *Forbes* (May 29), 137–38.

"How to Spot Defects in Business Brains," *Peoples Favorite Magazine* 33.5 (Nov.), 26–31.

"An Exotic Temple for a Chicago Suburb," *New York Times* (Aug. 1), 53.

1923

Business Practice Up to Date. Rochester, N.Y.: Business Ability Institute.

Correspondence Practice at Constable's, Rochester, N.Y.: The Business Ability Institute.

The Ideal Course in English for Vocational Students: Business Practice Up to Date, Or, How to Be a Private Secretary. Rochester, N.Y.: Business Ability Institute (2nd ed.).

Fundamentals of Business, by William Marvin Jackson, edited with exercises by Sherwin Cody. Rochester, N.Y.: Business Ability Institute.

Sherwin Cody's Business Ability Development Course. Rochester, N.Y.: The Business Ability Institute.

1924

Poe—Man, Poet, and Creative Thinker. New York: Boni and Liveright.

1927

An Evening with Twain. Rochester, N.Y.: Sherwin Cody School of English.

1928

The Sherwin Cody 100% Self-Correcting Course in Pronunciation, Accompanied by Sherwin Cody's Actual Voice Lessons in Six Parts (phonograph records). Rochester, N.Y.: The Sherwin Cody School of English.

1929

How to Speak and Write Masterly English. Rochester, N.Y.: The Sherwin Cody School of English.

1930

Habit-forming Language Practice, by Sherwin Cody, E.A. Cross, F.H. Bair, and Muriel Lanz. [Teachers' edition] Rochester, N.Y.: The Sherwin Cody School of English.

1933

The New Art of Writing and Speaking the English Language New York: Esser-Frederick [in six separate volumes which were collected as one in 1938 by the Sun Dial Press in New York].

1934

Interesting Letters, How to Write Them. New York & Chicago: The Gregg Publishing Company.
Teaching Letter Writing as a Composition Art: A Teacher's Manual for "Interesting Letters." New York & Chicago: The Gregg Publishing Company.

1937

Success in Letter Writing, Business and Social. Rochester, N.Y.: Sherwin Cody School of English.

1940

Pocket Cyclopedia of Good English. Rochester, N.Y.: Sherwin Cody School of English.

1944

Good English Quick Reference Book. New York: Good English Publishers.
Coaching Children in English. New York: Good English Publishers. [Includes *English in a Nutshell for Children* and tests of the Good English Institute.]

1950

Greatest Stories, and How They Were Written; selected by W. E. Henley with a series of introductions on the art of short story writing by Sherwin Cody. New York: Sherwin Cody Associates. [A re-edited version of Cody's 1902 *Selections from the World's Greatest Short Stories.*]

Letters: Writing to Get People to Do Things. Rochester, N.Y.: Sherwin Cody Course in English.

Bibliographic Note

This bibliography lists information for most but not all of Cody's publications, some of which are not recoverable: *Touch Typing-Writing Instructor, Business Letter Writing, Short Term Grammar Drill* (all cited in the 1907 edition of *Word-Study and Business Speller*), *Marshall Brown, American Business Man* (cited in *How to Deal with Human Nature in Business*), *Pitfalls in English* (advertised in a March 29, 1925 *New York Times* ad), *The Chinese Empire: Past and Present* (cited in the 1922 edition of *Story Writing and Journalism*), and *Language in a Nutshell for 100% Mastery* (cited in *Interesting Letters: How to Write Them*).

The Art of Writing & Speaking the English Language was first published in 1903 by Cody's Old Greek Press, in a Literary Digest edition and a "Special SYSTEM edition," and the same year in a revised edition by Funk & Wagnall's. The original series consisted of four books, *Word-study, Grammar and Punctuation, Composition,* and *Constructive Rhetoric. The Art of Writing & Speaking the English Language* was available as a boxed set (for $2) or individually (for 75¢ each).

Constructive Rhetoric reprinted *The Art of Short Story Writing* and *How to Write Fiction* and included some new material as well. *Constructive Rhetoric* was retitled *Story Writing and Journalism* in the 1905 Literary Digest edition, and the initial chapter on Business Letter Writing was removed to serve as the basis for "The Cody System" correspondence course).

The Funk & Wagnall's version was expanded to six volumes and included a volume on *The Dictionary of Errors* and *How to Read and What to Read,* the first volume of the Nutshell Library. G.P. Putnam's published a revised edition beginning in 1922 consisting of five books: *World-study, Grammar & Punctuation, Composition & Rhetoric, Constructive Rhetoric,* and *Dictionary of Errors.*

The New Art of Writing and Speaking the English Language was published in the 1930s, first by Esser, then by Sun Dial Press and Doubleday, and finally in the 1940s by Cody himself (Sherwin Cody Associates). The *New Art* included (as one volume) *Grammar, Punctuation, Word Study, Composition, Story Writing and Journalism, How to Do Business by Letter,* and *The Dictionary of Errors.*

Index